SHOP

HONG KONG

Fourth Edition

Bantam Books of Related Interest
Ask your bookseller for the books you have
  missed.

BORN TO SHOP: France
BORN TO SHOP: Italy
BORN TO SHOP: London
BORN TO SHOP: England, Scotland, and Ireland
BORN TO SHOP: Spain and Portugal
BORN TO SHOP: Hong Kong
BORN TO SHOP: New York
BORN TO SHOP: Los Angeles
BORN TO SHOP: Mexico
BORN TO SHOP: Florida

Born to
SHOP

HONG KONG

Fourth Edition

SUZY GERSHMAN
and
JUDITH THOMAS

Introduction by
DIANE FREIS

BANTAM BOOKS
NEW YORK • TORONTO • LONDON
SYDNEY • AUCKLAND

TO LIBBY HALLIDAY PALIN
one of our best finds ever

The currency used in Hong Kong is the Hong
Kong dollar, which is also signified by a dollar
sign. All prices quoted in this book are in U.S.
dollars unless otherwise noted. Although every
effort was made to ensure the accuracy of
prices appearing in this book, it should be
kept in mind that with inflation and a fluctuat-
ing rate of exchange, prices will vary. Dollar
estimations of prices were made based on the
following rate of exchange: $1 (U.S.) = $7 (H.K.).

BORN TO SHOP: HONG KONG

A Bantam Book / August 1986
Bantam Second Edition / February 1988
Bantam Third Edition / February 1990
Bantam Fourth Edition / November 1991

Produced by Ink Projects.
Design by Lynne Arany.
Maps by David Lindroth, Inc.

ISBN 0-553-35426-4

Published simultaneously in the United States and Canada

PRINTED IN THE UNITED STATES OF AMERICA

FG   0 9 8 7 6 5 4 3 2 1

The BORN TO SHOP Team

reported by:
Suzy Gershman
Aaron Gershman
editor: Jill Parsons
executive editor: Toni Burbank
assistant to executive editor: Linda Gross

CONTENTS

Preface

The book you have in your hands is the first post–Tiananmen Square edition of *Born to Shop: Hong Kong.* It is a very different book from our last edition because Hong Kong has changed so dramatically after the events of 1989 in China. It doesn't look much different; it simply feels different. And the shopping scene has changed too.

So welcome to a new edition that has been rewritten, reorganized, rechecked, and thoroughly reshopped to bring you up to date on one of our favorite cities.

One of the reporters for this book is a 10-year-old boy who had never been to the Orient before, and there is new information specially geared toward first-time tourists and children.

Shops in Hong Kong open and close at an amazing rate, so there is a chance that any given address may have changed since we went to press. If you are going out of your way for only one listing, we suggest you phone ahead. As with all our books, the same basic rules apply:

▼ No store can purchase a listing in this book or any book we write; we accept no advertising or paid announcements of any kind.

▼ Most of the stores never know we have "officially" visited them, no matter how many times we return.

▼ While our inside sources help to put us on the right track, we do visit each of their recommendations to see for ourselves.

▼ All opinions expressed are solely our own. We are very opinionated and outspokenly honest. Many guidebooks do not editorialize to the extent that we do.

▼ We do update the book regularly, but if you catch a change, please drop a card to *Born to Shop*, Bantam Books, 666 Fifth Avenue, 25th Floor, New York NY 10103.

▼ The turnover of stores is very high in Hong Kong; many don't go out of business but simply move to other locations. We have done our best, but please realize that—especially in Hong Kong—anything goes.

It is also our policy to mention brand names of goods we've seen in a store, but we cannot promise you that these same designer goods will be available in a certain store when you go there. "Now you see it, now you don't" is common practice in Hong Kong.

Acknowledgments

This brand-new edition is a major overhaul of our basic guide. With as many changes as we encounter in Hong Kong, we count on a lot of help from our friends.

We continue to work closely with the Hong Kong Tourist Association in New York and in Hong Kong. So big thanks to Mary Testa-Bakt and Edith Wei in New York, and to Stephen Wong, Winnie Fong, and Karisa Yuen-Ha Lui in Hong Kong. They have faxed and fact-checked and double-checked for us to make sure we've got things straight, and we thank them from the bottom of our shopping bags.

Morris Simoncelli at Japan Airlines continues as our basic host for both Hong Kong and Tokyo; we also thank Helen Coyle at JAL. We also want to send a big thank-you to United Airlines for letting us test the 747-400 from San Francisco.

Pacific Place, our travel brokers with the cheapest fares to the Orient, have great prices, fast service (even by mail), and entrée to all gateways. Many thanks to Lillian Fong there.

We have moved our shopping headquarters this year: On the Hong Kong Island side we are now enjoying the Mandarin Oriental Hotel, and we thank Geraldine Pitt for her extravagant hospitality. In Kowloon, we live at the Regent, where we are so spoiled by the service that we hate to leave our room to go shopping. Both Rose Kettle and Lynn Grebstad have gone out of their way to help us there; you'll find several of Rose's personal shopping tips woven into the text of this book. Thanks also to Patricia Dellegar in New York. When we've worn out our welcome at the Regent, we move over to the Ramada Renaissance, and we thank Judy Crawford for suggesting the hotel.

A revision such as this one is meaningless if you can't get down and dirty and talk it all out with your friends who really know the scene. For us, Hong Kong wouldn't be nearly so special if we couldn't spend time with local heroes Diane Freis, Peter Chan, and Richard Chen. Hugs to them and their families.

Finally, a big hug goes to Aaron Gershman, who went to Hong Kong and Tokyo instead of summer camp so he could do part of the work on this edition. Being with a 10-year-old gave a new perspective to the reporting.

Introduction

Welcome to Hong Kong, the crossroads of the world. All of the best things in life are here for your pleasure, and often at bargain prices. It's just a case of knowing where to look. Hong Kong is the world's best shopping center. There are world-class shopping malls. There are big-name boutiques that populate Kowloon and downtown Central.

Tourists come for the combination of hotels, local color, and shopping. And, hopefully, bargains.

Every commodity in the world is here in Hong Kong; shoppers never have to travel far to find bargains. The best part of all is that if one shop doesn't have what you want, the next one will . . . or the next.

Of course, half the fun of shopping in Hong Kong is bargaining. Everyone knows the price is negotiable, and it's a poor sport who doesn't go in prepared to argue.

Both Suzy and Judith are experts in finding the best bargains in town. They know this town better than many of the locals. I live here, but when they come to town and we sit down to visit, I invariably ask them for the latest secrets.

You may not develop an overnight love affair with Hong Kong as I did, but I promise you'll love the shopping.

Diane Freis

I ▾WELCOME TO HONG KONG

Enter Here

Hong Kong is known as the Gateway to the Orient because more people use it as their Asian base than any other city. Whether they visit on business or as tourists, they come to Hong Kong and then fan out, south to Bangkok or Singapore, west to China, or north toward Korea and Japan. Many will change planes in Japan on arrival in Asia, but they won't actually explore Japan until they are on their way home. Home from Hong Kong.

But today Hong Kong stands at a crossroads. No, we aren't referring to that day in 1997 when Hong Kong leaves British care and reverts to the Chinese. Oh no. The crisis came earlier for Hong Kong than it expected.

Tiananmen Square.

Tourists stopped flocking into China, lowering the number of passengers through Hong Kong. Yet Hong Kong rents did not fall, and so visitors were met by desperate retailers who could no longer afford to bargain, by high retail prices, and by a lack of shopping joy that permeated a depressed city.

And then it changed.

The dollar went to hell against European currencies. American tourists began to reconsider travel to Europe and suddenly took greater interest in the Orient. Because it is a big trip, Americans began to look at the big picture: several cities, business-class seats, luxury hotels and shopping—all booked in a spirit of adventure, because the dollar still goes so much farther in the Far East (except in Japan) than it does almost anywhere else.

So Hong Kong is redefining itself even as you read. It has stood on the brink of retail depression, of tourist suicide, and come back. The uncertainty of 1997 no longer seems so uncertain, because Hong Kong has survived 1990. Hong Kong is here to stay. Enter here and enjoy.

What about shopping in Hong Kong?

Well, it's changed a bit, but it's still great. That, too, is here to stay. We're going to show you the way.

Reference Points

When we refer to Hong Kong what we are talking about is the island itself, of course, but also Kowloon, the New Territories, and a few hundred islands. For the purposes of definition, we consider it all Hong Kong. In 1997 the British have to return both the island of Hong Kong and the New Territories to mainland China. In less than a decade, all that we refer to as Hong Kong will be considered part of the People's Republic of China (PRC). But that's another story.

Shopping in Hong Kong is concentrated heavily in two areas: Central, on the Hong Kong side, and Tsim Sha Tsui, in Kowloon. Central is very upscale, civilized, businesslike, and modern. Tsim Sha Tsui is more gritty, and more active in a frenetic way. There is more fashion in Central, but there are more deals to be had in Tsim Sha Tsui. Factory outlets are outside of the main shopping areas, in towns like Lai Chi Kok and Kwun Tong. These are all part of the Kowloon peninsula.

Both sides of the harbor are divided into distinct neighborhoods, each with its own personality. See Chapter 4 for a tour of the best shopping areas.

The Mostly Free Port of Hong Kong

Hong Kong did not become a shopper's mecca over a long span of time or because of the industrialization of the world. It was *created* to be a shopping paradise, for very real economic reasons. "Hong Kong isn't a city, it's a shopping mart," one observant soul said back in the late 1800s. Hong Kong is a capitalist's dream: There is duty on only a handful of commodities, and no duty on outgoing goods.

Because Hong Kong is an almost free port, most goods come in without taxation. For example, take your basic Chanel suit. Made in France, the suit costs *x francs* in France. When it's shipped to the United States, the price goes up because of shipping costs, and because the U.S. government levies high taxes against items that are competitive with U.S.-made goods. Since you can be very happy in an American-made suit, the duty on the Chanel suit is about 33%. Very steep! Send that same suit to Hong Kong and you have only shipping costs—there is no duty whatsoever. This does not mean that Chanel suits are a bargain in Hong Kong (they aren't—but for other reasons). This is just to explain the system in its basic form.

But the system has been changing in recent years; Hong Kong now has duty on perfumes and cosmetics. We were never that impressed with prices on these items anyway, but now they should be bought either at DFS stores (see page 187) or as you leave, in the duty-free store at the airport, where there is a huge makeup department. Prices on cosmetics are not dirt cheap, merely competitive with other duty-free prices around the world and slightly lower than at home.

The most interesting shopping news, for those

who don't care about price, is that despite this new duty Hong Kong continues to bring in new European products, so that you can find items here many months before they make their American debut. We were intrigued by the Sonia Rykiel makeup, certainly nowhere to be found in our local mall, but still couldn't bring ourselves to spend $27 (U.S.) on a lipstick!

But that's the story of business in Hong Kong these days. There are many choices, and many of them are sensational. But true bargains can be hard to spot.

A Short History of Hong Kong Trade

I f you've read or seen *Shōgun* or *Tai-Pan,* you're going to be one step ahead of us on this, but here goes. The Hong Kong area has always been a hotbed of commerce, because China silk came out of either Canton or Shanghai. Let's step back in time to the middle 1600s. You remember the Portuguese and their "black ship"? The black ship brought goods from Europe in exchange for silk from China. This was a great business, and the Portuguese wanted it all to themselves. So did the British, the Spaniards, the French, and, later, the Americans.

The only problem was, the big British ships couldn't get into the shallow waters of Macao (the Portuguese port), which is somewhat closer to Canton. But they soon happily discovered that the perfect port was on the island of Hong Kong. So for no other reason than deep water, Hong Kong became the "in" place. Queen Victoria howled with laughter when in 1842 Hong Kong was given to the British as a prize of war.

It was really a laughing matter. You see, not

only were silks and woolens being traded, there also was a thriving business in opium. The first Opium War ended with the British winning and getting Hong Kong, in perpetuity. The second and third times they won, they got the rights to Kowloon and then certain mainland territories for ninety-nine years. Back then, ninety-nine years sounded like a darn long time. However, in June of 1997, that ninety-nine–year lease is up, and those territories will go back to China on July 1. Stay tuned.

The Yin and Yang of Shopping

In the old days, shopping fever swept Hong Kong, and a certain excess of energy permeated the air. That was the 1980s. Things are different now that Hong Kong is just regaining its shopping feet. Some days you'll hit a lode and it will be just like your wildest dreams (if you are a first-timer), or just like the old days (if you are a repeat visitor). Other days, you'll find nothing.

We've been on the streets enough to know two important facts:

▼ The good stuff is often hidden. Either it's put away or it goes to those who have custom work done and know how to go after real value.

▼ You have to go back to the same places constantly and hope to get lucky. Or you have to hit it just right. It's just like shopping at Loehmann's (where you have come to accept the hit-or-miss philosophy).

It is virtually impossible to go to Hong Kong and not find anything to buy, but the days of deals galore may be over. The best value is represented by the tailor who custom-makes you a suit for the same price as an off-the-rack suit in the U.S., by the jeweler who creates one-of-a-kind jewelry for you at better-than-at-home prices, and by the street vendors who are selling their usual junk at prices low enough so you don't even care that they won't bargain.

If you look hard you can still get a name brand–style wristwatch for $15. And that Hermès-style handbag for $45 looks awfully good. And by the way, those double-strand matinee-length pearls we have cost only $40. The Gap shirts? Less than $10.

We can tell you that the Pedder Building, Central's most famous factory-outlet address, is in flux, and many showrooms in it are so disappointing that you are wasting your time trying to shop here. But in the same breath we must admit that while suffering the slings and arrows of the Pedder Building in order to research these changes, we also bought a designer knit dress for $20.

And that's the shopper's yin and yang.

When a Buy Is a Good-bye

A true-blue shopper has been known to lose her head now and again. And no place on earth is more conducive to losing one's head than Hong Kong. You can see so many great "bargains" that you end up buying many items just because the price is cheap, not because you need or want them. Or you can fall into the reverse trap, seeing nothing to buy, getting frustrated, and buying the wrong things. When you get home, you realize that you've tied up a fair amount of money in rather silly purchases. We've made so many mistakes, in fact, that we've had to have a long and careful talk with ourselves to come up with an out-of-town shopping philosophy that lays down the ground rules.

Shopping in a foreign country is much more romantic than shopping at home, there's no question about it. And, face it, most people expect to shop in Hong Kong. Even non-shoppers want to shop when away from home; they, too, love Hong Kong. But if you make a mistake while shopping in another American city, you can usually return the merchandise and get a credit with just a small amount of hassle. On a foreign trip, returns can be a major problem and usually aren't worth the effort. So, to keep mistakes to a minimum, we have our own rules of the game:

▼ Take a careful and thorough survey of your closet (including china and linen) and your children's closets before you leave town. Know what you've got so you can know what you need. While you don't have to need something in order to buy it, knowing that you need it (and will be saving money by buying it abroad) will help your conscience a lot.

▼ If you *need* an item of clothing to complete an ensemble, bring a piece of the outfit with you. (At the very least, very carefully cut a small swatch of fabric from the inside of the hem or a seam.)

▼ If you are planning on having an item made to fill a hole in your wardrobe, bring the other parts of the ensemble with you. If you expect to be 100% satisfied with anything you have custom-made in Hong Kong, you have to put 100% effort into your side of the deal. Show your tailor the suit that the blouse is supposed to go with.

▼ Figure the price accurately. Despite rumor to the contrary, the Hong Kong dollar *does* fluctuate!

▼ Figure in the duty. Each person is allowed $400 duty-free. If you are traveling with your family, figure out your family total. Children, even infants, still get the $400 allowance. If you have more than $400 worth of merchandise, you pay a flat 10% on the next $1,000; after that you pay according to various duty rates.

▼ Will you have to schlepp the item all over the world with you? If it takes up a lot of suitcase room, if it's heavy, if it's cumbersome, if it's breakable and at risk every time you pack and unpack or check your suitcase, if it has to be handheld—it might not be worth the cheap price tag. Estimate your time, trouble, and level of tolerance per item. Sure, it may be inexpensive, but if it's an ordeal to bring it home, is it really a good buy?

▼ Likewise, if you have to insure and ship it, is it still a bargain? How will you feel if the item never makes it to your door?

▼ Do your research on prices at home first. We spent several hours choosing and shipping lamps from a factory-outlet source only to discover an American discounter who, once the price of the shipping was taken into account, charged the same price.

▼ We are ambivalent about the value of counterfeit merchandise and cannot advise you whether to buy it or to walk away from it. If you suspect an item to be a fake, you must evaluate if this is a good buy or a good-bye. Remember that fakes most certainly do not have the quality of craftsmanship that originals have. You may also be asked to forfeit the item at U.S. Customs or pay duty on the value of the real object. But you may have a lot of fun with your fakes.

▼ Our rule of thumb on a good buy is that 50% (or more) off the U.S. price is a valuable saving. We think that a saving of less than 20% is marginal, is not worth the effort (of course, it depends on the item and how it will come back into the country with you, etc.), and is usually not a good buy. If the saving is 20% to 50%, we judge according to personal desire and the ratio of the previous points. If the saving is 50% or better, we usually buy several and whoop with joy. That's a good buy!

The Bed N Bath Rule of Shopping

We had one goal firmly in mind as we headed for Hong Kong: the master bedroom—pale yellow walls, Pierre Deux curtains, Victorian whitework in shams and duvet. What better place to buy a duvet cover, or two? (Need a spare while one's in the wash, right? They should be cheap in Hong Kong, right? Two for the price of one—let's be practical—right?)

So we scoured the streets of Hong Kong, of Kowloon, of Stanley. Duvet covers—and not even in styles we would kill for—cost in the $200–$300 (U.S.) range! We kept searching throughout the trip, but without success. Upon return to suburbia, we bopped right into the local branch of Bed N Bath and found, live from Shanghai, a set including queen-sized duvet cover, dust ruffle, and two pillow shams for $149.

The moral of the story: You may find Chinese-made products are cheaper at home than in Hong Kong.

The Bed N Bath Rule of Shopping/ Part 2

A few days after return from Hong Kong, we received in the mail a catalogue from the department store I. Magnin, in California. In this small but densely packed fanfare of merchandise was a very good selection of the same items found in any international duty-free store. The $470 Gucci watch that seemed like a bargain in the duty-free in Hong Kong cost only $495 from I. Magnin.

If possible, try to get your hands on prices and pictures of the kind of merchandise that interests you, so you can decide if there really are savings to be had. The Magnin catalogue had goodies from Fendi, Chanel, Gucci, Ferragamo, etc. Call toll-free for your own copy: (800) 227-1125.

Be Prepared

U nless you are used to traveling in the Far East, you will find Hong Kong extremely different from anything you've ever seen before. Depending on how sheltered your life has been, you may even go into culture shock. We don't preach about politics or the poor, but we do suggest that you be mentally prepared for what you are about to experience. There are a few particularly important cultural details:

▼ Chinese street vendors and retailers may be rude to Anglos. We try not to generalize about a thing like this, but you'll soon discover it is a common thread of conversation among tourists and expats alike.

▼ The system is greased by "tea money"—tip everyone and anyone if you want favors, information, or even a smile.

▼ Times have been tough since Tiananmen Square. Many retailers now refuse to bargain.

▼ As a tourist, you will never get the cheapest price possible, so forget it.

▼ You are a rich American and will never miss what you overpay, according to many vendors. Some of these people want to make enough money to immigrate before 1997—watch out!

2 ▾ DETAILS

Information Please

How to, where to, and what to are the questions everyone asks when planning a trip to Hong Kong. No other Asian city has the choices Hong Kong offers in hotels, transportation, and shopping. As a result, just planning the trip can be an adventure. Everyone has his favorite places to recommend. Listen to them all, then make your own lists. We have compiled ours from listening to scads of expats, locals, and experts and then seeing for ourselves.

Hong Kong is an easy city to negotiate once you know the system. Spend some time with maps before you go and you will hit the streets running. Don't be afraid of the language barrier.... Most Chinese retailers in Hong Kong understand some English, either written or spoken. Carry your hotel's card with you, with addresses in Chinese in case you end up in the New Territories or at outlying factory outlets and need directions home. Outside of the main shopping districts, there may be fewer people who speak or understand English, but there are plenty of folks who are willing to try to help you out.

The times we've had trouble getting a point across or giving directions we found that simply writing out your question or the address is helpful for the person you are talking to. Often, it's not that they don't understand English, it's just that they are having difficulty understanding your accent.

Hong Kong for Kids

Although we had never thought of Hong Kong as the perfect place for a family vacation, we were shocked at how much fun we had with child in tow and how different Hong Kong looked in the company of a kid. Even if your child hates to shop at home, he just may catch the bug in Hong Kong. It's likely he'll pan the Toys "Я" Us if he's got one at home (this one is not very large by suburban American standards) but will flip out for Japanese department stores, street vendors, Whimseyland (in many shopping malls), and the parlors where video games are played for the equivalent of pennies (although the signs usually say children must be 16 or over to play, our reporter had no trouble).

Hotels are air-conditioned and offer American movies (free) on television; they usually have pools and baby-sitting service. There are American fast-food joints galore; most hotels have spaghetti on the menu. Even the snazzy Regent Hotel, where you might be reluctant to take a child, offers an American-style hot dog for lunch along with its incredible view.

Don't miss Stanley Market, the sampans of Aberdeen, the Space Museum, a ride on a tram, a ride on the Star Ferry, the Bird Market, a movie in Chinese. And plenty of shopping. Give your kids $50 (H.K.) and they will feel like a million. Some of the things they might want to buy (or you can buy as gifts to bring home) include straw coolie hats ($4); satin mandarin caps with long black braided pigtails made of yarn ($4); cloisonné rings ($1.25); T-shirts ($1.25); calculators inset into a fake piece of folded currency, your choice among many international currencies ($1–$5); and video games ($10–$40).

Booking Hong Kong / 1

Most Hong Kong guidebooks are the standard texts containing information on where to stay, what to eat, and which sights to see. Take your choice. Our favorites are those put out by the Hong Kong Tourist Association. You can pick up a packet full of brochures published by the HKTA as you exit passport control at Hong Kong International Airport. If you visit HKTA's main counter at Jardine House, 1 Connaught Place, Central, on the 35th floor, you can pick up a more complete selection. HKTA publishes three pamphlets that we consider a must: *The Official Guide to Shopping, Eating Out and Services in Hong Kong* gives you the address of every HKTA member shop by area and by category. While they do not recommend one shop over another, they at least have elicited a promise from their member shops to be honest. If they are not, you have the HKTA on your side. Look for their listings of factory outlets that are members of the association. Addresses are given in both English and Chinese. The *Official Hong Kong Guide* is published monthly and contains general information about the city. The HKTA also publishes a weekly newspaper. It contains news of events and shows, along with the usual ads for shops.

A magazine that we rely on is the *A-O-A Map Directory*. It is handed out free at the airport and at HKTA offices. Maps show both building and street locations. Since so many addresses include the building name, street, and area, it makes finding an address simple. For example, if you are looking for the Gucci shop in The Landmark on Des Voeux Road in Central, simply locate Des Voeux Road in Central on the map and find The Landmark Building. You then know the cross streets and surrounding points of reference.

Delta Dragon Publications has expanded its line of local guidebooks and publishes *Hong Kong Factory Bargains* and *Hong Kong Yin & Yang. Hong Kong Factory Bargains* is updated yearly and contains many factory-shop listings. If you are planning to be in the city for an extended period of time or are simply determined to hit all of the factory outlets (no matter how exhausting this may be), this is a useful book to have. Addresses are given in Chinese and English. *Hong Kong Yin & Yang* is a general guidebook.

Hong Kong Shopping Guide to Home Decorating by Barbara Anderson-Tsang and Leopoldine Arikula is a new shopping guide; note that it is geared to residents. It costs about $12 at bookstores and hotels.

Booking Hong Kong/2

Many tour companies and large hotel chains offer shopping packages for Hong Kong, but if you want to put together your own, we recommend some of our favorite shopping hotels that will put you in the heart of the action. Some are fancier than others. They are all convenient to the MTR (Hong Kong's subway system).

Some secrets that might make booking your hotel easier:

▼ Ask the hotels first if they are offering weekend or five-day rates. Almost all hotels discount rooms during the off season or when there is not a lot of business in town. Hong Kong has so many conventions, and so many new hotels, that you should be able to get a deal almost any time except for Chinese New Year.

▼ The Hong Kong Tourist Association publishes a brochure called *Hong Kong Hotel Guide*. Write to their head office in Chicago for a copy (HKTA, Suite 2400, 333 North Michigan Avenue, Chicago IL 60601). This publication provides a comprehensive list of all the possibilities, including addresses, phone numbers, room rates, fax numbers, and services offered.

▼ Check the big chains for promotional rates. Often you can prepay in U.S. dollars and save. Consider putting together your own group, and booking yourself as a tour package. Every hotel has a special department to deal with groups, and offers incentives.

▼ We rate hotels as inexpensive (under $100 per night), moderate ($100–$200 per night), and expensive (over $200 per night). All rates include government tax (5%) and hotel service charge (10%). We have listed our hotels together by area, on Hong Kong Island or in Kowloon. There are benefits to staying on either side of the harbor. If you have business in Central, you will probably want to be on the island. If you are here on holiday, and want easy access to the factory outlets, stay in Kowloon.

Shopping Hotels of Hong Kong

Central

MANDARIN ORIENTAL HOTEL: While Central is teeming with luxury hotels, the Mandarin Oriental has established itself as both the power hotel for businesspeople and the shopping hotel for those who want to be in the midst of the area's best stores. Located one block from either the Star Ferry or the

Central station of the MTR, the hotel has a shopping arcade with some of the best names in Hong Kong, and is also located across the street from the Prince's Building and a stone's throw from The Landmark and even the Pedder Building. Once you check in, a little old man comes to your room to perform a welcoming tea ceremony. U.S. reservations: (800) 663-0787. Expensive.

MANDARIN ORIENTAL HOTEL, 5 Connaught Road Central, Hong Kong (MTR: Central)

▼

HONG KONG MARRIOTT: One of the newest additions to the Hong Kong hotel race, the Marriott is not only gorgeous, it is also connected directly to one of the chicest shopping arcades in town. Completed in 1989, the 27-story tower has 564 guest rooms, an outdoor pool, fitness rooms, water views, and The Mall at Pacific Place underneath. It is located on a hill just east of the main Central shopping district, midway between the Hong Kong Convention Center and The Landmark. It is easy to reach via the Admiralty MTR. Since this is the Marriott's flagship hotel in Asia, it is guaranteed to be first-rate all the way. Reservations: (800) 228-9290. Expensive.

HONG KONG MARRIOTT, Pacific Place, 88 Queensway, Hong Kong (MTR: Admiralty)

▼

CONRAD HOTEL: While we've enjoyed ourselves at the Hong Kong Hilton in the past, the big Hilton news is their new chain of hotels called Conrad, after you know who. The new Conrad in Hong Kong is particularly jazzy: it's a tall monolith located next to the Marriott and across the courtyard from The Mall at Pacific Place. It's meant to be a business hotel and amenities are structured for the businessperson, but this is a pretty good shopping location as well. U.S. reservations: (800) HILTONS. Expensive.

CONRAD HOTEL, 2 Queen's Road Central, Hong Kong (MTR: Admiralty)

Kowloon

THE REGENT HOTEL: Still considered to be one of the most scenic locations in Hong Kong, the Regent occupies the tip of Kowloon Peninsula, and the views from the lobby bar at night are nothing short of spectacular.

We once got upgraded to a suite that had a whirlpool bath situated against a huge glass wall so you could luxuriate in the tub and watch the Star Ferry float across the harbor. The room also had its own sauna, and a wall of glass to maximize the view. But view is not all the Regent is about: They have the town's best hotel shopping mall, which has replaced the one at The Peninsula Hotel as the chicest address. Every big-name European designer has a shop here, but other big names abound— from Diane Freis to Donna Karan! If that isn't enough, there's also a less fancy mall (New World Shopping Centre) attached to the Regent's three-level mall.

Part of what's so interesting about this hotel is that it is both formal and casual at the same time. While the Mandarin Oriental Hotel reeks of power and prestige, this hotel radiates luxe and leisure, even to businesspeople. U.S. reservations: (800) 545-4000. Expensive.

THE REGENT HOTEL, Salisbury Road, Kowloon (MTR: Tsim Sha Tsui)

▼

RAMADA RENAISSANCE HOTEL: The Ramada Renaissance is well located for all the action in Kowloon. It is directly opposite the sprawling Harbour City complex, a five-minute walk to the Tsim Sha Tsui MTR stop or the Star Ferry, and a two-second walk to the heart of Kowloon shopping. The hotel is spanking clean, and has larger-than-usual rooms. There are gourmet restaurants and an attached shopping arcade (Sun Plaza). The hotel is especially well designed for the businessperson, with speaker-equipped telephones and personal-computer outlets in all rooms. The Business Center has fax machines, laptops with software, and VCRs for rent. They offer a fitness center and a large indoor swimming pool. The Ramada Renaissance was sold to the owners of the New World Hotels, but Ramada continues to manage the property. Reservations: (800) 228-2828. Moderate.

RAMADA RENAISSANCE HOTEL, 8 Peking Road, Kowloon (MTR: Tsim Sha Tsui)

▼

HYATT REGENCY HONG KONG: The epitome of a shopping hotel. The lobby is directly above the shopping arcade. The arcade has been renovated and now houses some very chic designer shops. The hotel is a popular tour-group choice because of its convenient location and price. There are 706 rooms, all with shopping views. Reservations: (800) 338-9000. Moderate.

HYATT REGENCY HONG KONG, 67 Nathan Road, Kowloon (MTR: Tsim Sha Tsui)

▼

OMNI THE HONG KONG HOTEL: Harbour City has three hotels built in and around its office and shopping complex; we like this one the best. It is the closest to Ocean Terminal and has a mezzanine that is devoted to antiques shops. The lobby design is modern chic, and the rooms overlook either the harbor or the shopping. The other hotels also run by Omni are the Omni Marco Polo Hotel and the Omni Prince Hotel. Reservations: (800) 448-8355. Inexpensive.

OMNI THE HONG KONG HOTEL, Harbour City, 2 Canton Road, Kowloon (MTR: Tsim Sha Tsui)

Getting There

When it comes to booking your plane tickets, have we got news for you. You can do it the regular way, or you can get a deal. We love to fly Japan Air Lines, and find that their service is tops. JAL flies out of New York, Los Angeles, Chicago, and San Francisco, as well as fifty-six other cities in thirty-three countries. Their package tours and special fares make them unbeatable. In the continental United States call (800) 525-3663. Or, in New York call (212) 838-4400; in Chicago (312) 565-7000; in San Francisco (415) 982-8141.

Flights on all airplanes to Hong Kong, especially from the East Coast, are packed. One of the reasons for this is that there are wholesalers who buy blocks of tickets, knowing they will be able to resell them to travel agents and tour groups. Because they buy in bulk, they get a better price. These ticket brokers pass the savings on to their customers. Our friend Libby, who travels frequently back and forth to Hong Kong, introduced us to Lillian Fong. Lillian and her comrades are ticket brokers for many airlines to many destinations. We have used her to book tickets to Hong Kong and Europe, and find that her prices are hard to beat. You can book any class of service; Lillian will tell you the airline and time when you can get the best deal. The seats are legitimate. They have nothing to do with coupons or other questionable practices. Call her and tell her we sent you, since her business is otherwise in wholesale blocks. Lillian will also assemble tours into China or other Asian destinations. Be sure to ask. It is usually cheaper to book a package, which includes room, breakfast, and all taxes, than to just purchase the airfare. You may also want to book an around-the-world ticket, which is sometimes a bargain. This is handy for those who want to see a lot of the Orient and still save money. Call or fax Lillian Fong, Pacific Place Travel, 7540A East Garvey, Rosemead, CA 91770. Telephone: (818) 307-3218; fax: (818) 307-3223.

If you are leaving from the West Coast, look into one of aviation's newest treats: a plane that flies nonstop from there to Hong Kong. The flight takes about fourteen hours, but you don't have to lay over at Narita. (If you want to get to Narita, it's only ten hours from the West Coast!) You also have less jet lag!

We've happily tested United Airlines from San Francisco. While it can be a long haul if you are connecting directly from the East Coast, the flight is a breeze if you lay over at an airport hotel or visit friends/do business on the West Coast before continuing. Of course, if you start on the West Coast you'll never fly any other plane.

Since we've now gotten to be old China hands at getting back and forth, we have a few tips to save you some money:

▼ Look into what is called a Circle Pacific fare. Most American carriers, and many other internationals, offer you this chance to make your own itinerary but to travel to several cities in the Orient at package-tour prices. You do not join a group; you set your own pace, but you get a break on the price because you fly all legs with the same carrier.

▼ Don't be afraid of business class. The trip is a lengthy one; you will be much more comfortable in business class. Furthermore, there are more business class seats than any other (you aren't the only person who really doesn't want to do this trip in a coach seat), so there are more deals than you thought. We had the shock of a lifetime when we priced out Aaron Gershman's ticket. The business-class child fare was only $200 more than the economy ticket! Our JAL plane, a 747, comprised a small first-class section up front and a small coach section upstairs. The rest of the plane was business class.

▼ Package tours often offer you the best deals, especially if they include airport transfers and some extras.

Don't overlook international carriers as a good source of information and packages. Note that direct service does not mean that the airplane does not stop; it simply means that you will be booked straight through. Some West Coast flights do not stop; others do.

Getting Around

E ven though everywhere you look in Hong Kong you will see signs in Chinese, and everywhere you walk you will hear people speaking Chinese, you will have no trouble getting around. Often the people speaking Chinese also speak, read, or understand English, and the signs that you can't read at first probably have the information somewhere in English—just smaller. Hong Kong has been a British colony for so long that English is a second language. Most cab drivers speak and understand English. Always travel with a map, in case you need to point to where you want to go, or if you are merely wandering around and simply want to get your bearings.

Mass transportation in Hong Kong is superb. Most rides on the MTR take under twenty minutes. Crossing the harbor by car or cab during rush hour is hardest, but doing it on the Star Ferry or the MTR is a breeze. If you intend to sightsee, pick up the HKTA brochure *Places of Interest by Public Transportation* to get exact directions and bus routes throughout Hong Kong Island and Kowloon. There are many ways to get around.

AIRPORT TRANSPORTATION: Getting to your hotel from Kai Tak International Airport can be accomplished via bus or taxi. The airport bus provides access to many major hotels. Fares run about $6 (H.K.) to Tsim Sha Tsui hotels and $8 (H.K.) to Hong Kong Island hotels. Take bus A1 for Tsim Sha Tsui, A2 for Central and Wanchai, and A3 for Causeway Bay. Buses run every fifteen minutes from 7 A.M. until 11 P.M. Check to make certain that your hotel is on the list.

Most hotels will send a special car or bus to pick you up. The Regent has a fleet of Daimlers. The Peninsula has Rolls Royces. A driver will meet you outside Customs and help you with your luggage. This is extra, but after a long flight the service is worth it: expect round-trip hotel car service to be added to your bill. The price is about $50 round-trip; you do not tip the driver. This is $50 (U.S.), not (H.K.).

Taxi stands are near the arrival lounge. A large sign will give you approximate fares to different areas of Hong Kong and Kowloon. If you are confused, look for the transportation desk across from the arrival doors. The staff there will help you find the best means of transportation to your hotel. Don't forget to stop by the HKTA desk to pick up their free brochures on the city.

MTR: The Mass Transit Railway (MTR) makes going anyplace in Hong Kong a delight. Look for the symbol 木, which marks the MTR station. Three lines connect the New Territories to industrial Kwun Tong to business Central to shopping Tsim Sha Tsui to the residential eastern part of the island.

The longest trip takes less than sixty minutes, and the cost of the ticket is based on distance. You buy your ticket at the station vending machines by looking for your destination and punching in the price code. You will need exact change, which you can get from a change machine nearby. There are also ticket windows where you can buy multiple tickets. If you are visiting Hong Kong from overseas, the best value is a $20 (H.K.) tourist MTR ticket, which can be obtained from any HKTA office, MTR station, select Hang Seng Banks, or MTR Travel Services Centres. You must buy your ticket within two weeks of your arrival and show your passport at the time you purchase it. With this ticket you can ride for $20 (H.K.) worth of travel on the MTR and get your last ride anywhere in the system even if you do not have enough value left.

If you are unclear about how the system works, pick up a copy of the MTR guidebook at any station ticket office, or telephone 750-0170, which is the MTR Passenger Enquiry Hotline.

Remember to keep your ticket after you enter the turnstile, because you will have to reinsert it to exit. If you get off at the wrong stop and owe more money, the machine will let you know.

The MTR runs between 6 A.M. and 1 A.M. If you need to get somewhere earlier or later, take a taxi.

BUSES: Hong Kong's bus routes can also get you just about anywhere you might want to go. Most of the buses are double-deckers and provide a great way to see the city as you ride.

China Motor Bus runs Hong Kong Island's cream-and-blue buses, and Kowloon Motor Bus operates the cream-and-red ones. Bus stops are marked with a large disc on a pole containing the numbers of buses that stop there. You need exact change to take the buses, which can be a pain if you don't know where you are going or how much it costs. Always carry extra change and simply point to your destination on a map. The bus drivers are friendly and will help. If they are too busy, a fellow rider will fill in. The most expensive bus ride is $7 (H.K.). Buses operate from 6 A.M. until midnight daily. The main bus terminals in Central are below Exchange Square and next to the Macao Ferry Pier on Connaught Road; in front of Wanchai Ferry Pier; and in front of the North Point Ferry Pier. If you're traveling from Kowloon, the main bus terminals are in front of the Star Ferry, Jordan Ferry, and Tai Kok Tsui Ferry terminals. Signs are in English and Chinese. The HKTA publishes a brochure giving bus routes.

MINIBUSES AND MAXICABS: These sixteen-seat vehicles travel some of the same routes as the double-decker buses. They are not as easy to use unless you already know your way around. The red-and-yellow ones are called Minibuses. To get one to stop, yell *"Yau lok!"* You pay as you get off, depending on the distance you have traveled. The green-and-yellow buses, called Maxicabs, follow more distinct routes. You can take these to the Peak, Ocean Park, Aberdeen, and other tourist locations. You pay a fixed price based on destination as you get on. Main terminals are beside the Star Ferry terminal in Hong Kong (for Ocean Park) or beside City Hall (for the Peak).

TAXIS: Finding a taxi in Hong Kong is like finding one in any major city (except L.A.)— just raise your hand. If the taxi is free, it will have a raised flag, or the sign on top will be lit. As you enter the taxi, the meter will start, with an immediate charge of $8 (H.K.). From then on the charge is $1 (H.K.) per quarter kilometer. Taking the Cross-Harbour Tunnel will cost an extra $10 (H.K.) for the cab to return; crossing costs $10 (H.K.), making the total additional fees $20 (H.K.). There are surcharges for luggage ($2 H.K. per piece), waiting time, and radio calls. If a taxi is in Central and has a sign saying "Kowloon," it means that the driver wants a fare going back to Kowloon and will not charge the extra $10 (H.K.) tunnel fee. Shift changes occur at 4 P.M., and it is sometimes hard to find a cab. If a taxi doesn't stop for you on a busy road, it is probably because he is not allowed to. Look for a nearby tax⁚ stand where you can pick up a cab. Hotels are always good places to find a taxi. Even if you are not staying at that particular hotel, the doorman will help you and appreciate your tip. Taxis in the New Territories and on the island of Lantau have slightly cheaper fares.

TRAINS: The Kowloon-Canton railway system services the areas between Hung Hom and the Chinese border, where you can change trains and continue into the People's Republic of China, and on to the USSR and London. There are two main service routes: the daily express for those going to the People's Republic, and the commuter train for those who wish to sightsee or commute. The final stop is at Lo Wu, and you must have a visa to continue from there.

FERRIES: The most famous of all Hong Kong ferries is the Star Ferry, with service from Kowloon to Central and back. The eight-minute ride is one of the most scenic in the world. You can see the splendor of Hong Kong Island's architecture and the sprawl of Kowloon's shore. The green-and-white ferries have been connecting the island to the peninsula since 1898.

Fares are still very affordable. First class (upper deck) is $2 (H.K.) and tourist class (lower deck) $1 (H.K.). The difference is minimal except at rush hour, when the upper deck is less crowded. The Central/Tsim Sha Tsui service runs from 6:30 A.M. to 11:30 P.M. There is also a ferry connecting Tsim Sha Tsui with Wanchai and the new convention facilities. This service operates between 7:30 A.M. and 11 P.M.

Other ferries connect Hong Kong with various outlying islands. The terminal is west of the Star Ferry terminal at the Outlying Districts Service Pier. Buy a round-trip ticket to save time and allow yourself to relax. The HKTA has a schedule of ferry service, or you can call the Yau Ma Tei Ferry Company at 542-3081.

TRAMS: Watch out crossing the streets of Central, or you are likely to be run over by a tram. Island trams have been operating for more than eighty-five years, running from the far western Kennedy Town to Shau Kei Wan in the east. They travel in a straight line except for a detour around Happy Valley. Fares are $.60 (H.K.) for adults and $.20 (H.K.) for children. Pay as you exit. Many trams do not go the full distance east to west, so note destination signs before getting on. Antique trams are available for tours and charters, as are the regular ones.

The Peak Tram has been in operation for more than 100 years. It is a must for any visitor to Hong Kong—unless you are afraid of heights. You can catch the tram behind the Hilton Hotel, on Garden Road. A free shuttle bus will take you from the Star Ferry or Central MTR station (Chater Garden exit) to the Peak Tram terminal. The tram runs to the Peak every ten minutes starting at 7 A.M. and ending at midnight. The trip takes eight minutes. At the top you hike around to various viewing points, or peek in on some of the expensive mansions and high rises. The best time to make this trip is just before dusk; you can see the island scenery on the trip up, walk around and watch the spectacular sunset, then ride down as all the city lights are twinkling. The tram costs $10 (H.K.) round-trip or $6 (H.K.) one-way for adults and $4 (H.K.) round-trip for children.

RICKSHAWS: The few remaining rickshaws are lined up just outside of the Star Ferry terminal on Hong Kong Island. No new rickshaw licenses have been granted since 1972, and the gentlemen who still hold their licenses have been pulling rickshaws for some years. Rarely, if ever, do people actually go for a ride around Central. Most people just want to have their pictures taken. The cost for a ride or picture is negotiable. Pictures should cost around $10–$20 (H.K.), and a ride around the block $50 (H.K.). Your kids will beg you for a ride or a photo; the rickshaw drivers will milk you for top price. And yet ask your children about their best memories of Hong Kong and they will cite the rickshaw encounter.

CAR RENTAL: Avis, Budget, and Hertz have offices in Hong Kong if you want to drive yourself. You must be 18 or older and hold a valid driver's license or international driver's permit. We think that driving around Hong Kong is more work than pleasure. Hotels offer a car and driver for an hourly rate, which varies depending on the hotel and car. Check the concierge desk before committing to either.

CAR HIRE: It's unlikely that you'll want to drive in Hong Kong, but you should seriously consider hiring a car for a day or a portion of a day. Most hotels offer this service; some have various types of cars with different price points. (The Benz is less than the Rolls.) The price includes a tip; at $40 (H.K.) an hour you can see a lot of Hong Kong and save time by getting to hard-to-reach places that would eat up your day via public transportation. We did a good bit of our research for this edition with the help of a car and driver—nervously looking at watches and wondering if we would have to rob a bank. We zipped along quickly (knowing the driver was waiting cut down on the shopping time at each stop), and felt the investment was worthwhile.

HYDROFOIL AND JETFOIL: Those traveling to Macao will want to know about the hydrofoil and jetfoil service, which runs every hour between 7 A.M. and 1 A.M. from the Macao Ferry Pier in the west end of the Central District. Less frequently, but often enough to be convenient, there is direct service from the Hong Kong China City terminal in Kowloon. The trip takes a little under an hour, with jetfoils being slightly faster than hydrofoils. Since Macao is a Portuguese colony, you must bring your passport and pay a $20 (H.K.) exit tax.

Snack and Shop

I t's quite easy to get a snack in Hong Kong. It's simply a question of how adventurous you are. One of us doesn't hesitate to eat from street stands; the other needs white linen. The salads in a good hotel restaurant should be fine. We don't drink the water in quantity.

Experiment as much as you wish. We offer a few suggestions for fun, inexpensive, colorful stops that won't take much time and are convenient to most of your shopping trips. If you're out shopping at the factory outlets in the outlying areas you may want to bring along a picnic lunch, or at least something to drink. There are a few fast-food and local shops mixed in among the factory buildings, but the less adventurous traveler will probably be happier with a packed lunch.

There are more and more franchised American fast-food joints in Hong Kong. We can report complete satisfaction with Kentucky Fried Chicken, but must also say there are no Chicken McNuggets in Hong Kong (they have them in Tokyo), and McDonald's did not please our expert. Pizza Hut was also a bust (for the expert, anyway).

One of our best tricks is to eat in hotels so we can look around, get a feel of the crowd and the action, and get off our feet. You can have all the magnificence of the Regent and its glorious view from the coffee shop, where you can get a hot dog for $4. This happens to be the deal of the century. And the hot dog complied with the standards of our expert. The coffee shop is downstairs from the lobby; walk toward the wall of glass, past check-in, and go down the stairs to your left. The Peninsula Hotel, which used to be a must for tea (the Regent has replaced the Peninsula, and now it's best for drinks in the lobby bar), does have spaghetti for lunch or dinner; you can eat a meal for $10.

You might also want to try:

ITALIAN TOMATO TOKYO: We know this sounds like the wrong shop in the wrong town, but trust us. . . . Located directly across Canton Road from Harbour City, this fast-food restaurant is part of the Mitsukoshi department store. The Silvercord Building is to the right as you exit. Italian Tomato Tokyo offers both Chinese and Italian fast food. We like the pizza, the spaghetti, or the noodles, although you can get much fancier meals as well. The decor is crisp and clean; service is fast and prices are inexpensive.

ITALIAN TOMATO TOKYO, Sun Plaza Arcade, 28 Canton Road, Kowloon (MTR: Tsim Sha Tsui)

SUN TUNG LOK SHARKS FIN RESTAU-RANT: You can't leave Hong Kong without *dim sum* and then some shark's fin soup. This is our favorite spot for both, located at the far end of the Harbour City complex, in the Ocean Galleries. The atmosphere is noisy and the restaurant is always crowded. It will take a couple of trips to taste all the varieties of seafood offered, and have *dim sum* too.

SUN TUNG LOK SHARKS FIN RESTAURANT, Harbour City/Ocean Galleries, 25–27 Canton Road, Kowloon (MTR: Tsim Sha Tsui)

▼

FOOD STREET: If you are in Causeway Bay and in need of a quick bite, there is no easier place to stop than along Food Street. This pedestrian arcade is lined with predominantly Chinese restaurants. Entry to Food Street is from either Gloucester Road or Kingston Street, one block west of Victoria Park. This is next to The Excelsior Hotel. If you can't choose on your own, we suggest Riverside Cafe for *dim sum*.

FOOD STREET, Gloucester Road, Hong Kong (MTR: Causeway Bay)

Hours

Shops open late and stay open late. The majority of specialty stores open at 9:30 A.M. and close at 6:30 P.M. However, these are just general guidelines; depending on the area, there are stores opening as late as 10 or 11 A.M. and closing as late as 11 P.M. Many of the stores don't open as early as they say they will. Most shops in the main shopping areas of Tsim Sha Tsui and Causeway Bay are open seven days a week. Those in Central close on Sunday.

Major public holidays are honored in many shops. Everything closes on Chinese New Year. Do not plan to be in Hong Kong and do any shopping at this time. The stores that remain open charge a premium. The stores where you want to shop will all be closed.

Store hours are affected by the following public holidays: January 1 (New Year's Day); January/February (Chinese New Year); March/April (Good Friday, Easter Sunday and Monday); June (Dragon Boat Festival); August 25 (Liberation Day); December 25 (Christmas); and December 26 (Boxing Day). On public holidays banks and offices close, and there is a higher risk of shops closing as well. Factory outlets will definitely not be open. Many holiday dates change from year to year. For specific dates contact the HKTA before you plan your trip.

If you are planning a tour of the factory outlets remember that lunch hour is anywhere from noon to 2 P.M., although 1 P.M. to 2 P.M. is most common. Outlet shops will close for one hour along with the factory. You might as well plan to have lunch then too.

Department-store hours differ from store to store. The larger ones, like Lane Crawford and Chinese Arts & Crafts, maintain regular business hours, 10 A.M. to 5 or 6 P.M. The Japanese department stores in Causeway Bay open between 10 and 10:30 A.M. and close between 9 and 9:30 P.M. They have alternating closing days, however, that can be confusing.

Made in Hong Kong

I f it is "Made in Hong Kong" is it cheaper in Hong Kong? The answer to this is yes—and no. A shirt manufactured in Hong Kong and sold in Hong Kong is going to cost less than the same shirt sold in New York. First of all, in Hong Kong there is no shipping; and second, there is no duty. However, the big-name designers don't care. Manufacturing has become so sophisticated that goods can be cut in China, assembled in Hong Kong, and finished in France.

There is one other caveat about those famous words "Made in Hong Kong." Just because an item is made there does not mean you will find it in local stores or outlets. Many garments are shipped direct to the overseas stores, with only dust left behind in the warehouse.

Toys, which are made in Hong Kong, are sent out to be packaged and therefore are imported back into Hong Kong at prices pretty close to those at home. Don't expect any great deals. There are some savings on Nintendo (see page 232).

European-made Bargains

T here are no European-made bargains in Hong Kong. OK, there may be several if you run into a big sale period. But for the most part, it is wrong to assume that Hong Kong prices are cheaper than U.S. prices on expensive European-made designer goods.

If you see merchandise that you always thought was made in Europe, and it's very inexpensive in Hong Kong, you may be thinking that we are crazy and don't know what we are talking about. We are not, and we do. No matter what the label says, the goods were made in Hong Kong.

Hong Kong on Sale

Hong Kong has two traditional sale periods, the end of August and shortly before Chinese New Year (January-February).

Aside from European merchandise, everything else goes on sale during this same period. What you'll find is a lot of no-name merchandise that didn't interest you when it cost $50 (U.S.) but is looking a lot better when it's marked down to $30.

The best thing about the sales in Hong Kong is that this is your best time to get regular retail merchandise at its lowest price. The real bargains in Hong Kong are not in retail stores; the real bargains in Hong Kong may not be in perfect condition. So if you insist on brand-new, clean, undamaged goods, you should feel safe buying them on sale. If you have teens or are on a limited clothing budget, shop Hong Kong during the sale periods. Check the *South China Morning Post* ads for special sale announcements.

Remember, the best buys in Hong Kong are not in retail shops—so, to us, whether you are there for a sale period or not is meaningless.

Taxing Thoughts

R ecently added U.S. luxury taxes require those who buy fur and jewelry to pay tax on big-ticket items. You cannot actually bypass this tax by buying these same luxury items in Hong Kong, because the duty on them will come out more or less the same. However, if you are traveling with your family and you combine your duty-free allowance, you can reduce the amount of duty that is paid—depending, of course, on how many family members are with you and the total amount of your purchases abroad. The duty on fur is very low, so that Hong Kong remains a great place to buy a mink coat.

Typhoon Retailing

D uring the summer (from May to September), Hong Kong falls prey to typhoons. To protect the population best, the Royal Observatory now ranks the typhoons in numerical order, going up from 1 to 10. While each number has some significance in terms of the velocity of the wind, we will translate this to you only in terms of shopping habits.

No. 3 typhoon: The Star Ferry might stop running.

No. 8 typhoon: All stores are supposed to close; everyone is supposed to go home or seek shelter. Offices will not be open during a No. 8. *However,* hotel stores will stay open and may even jack up their prices.

Tourists are told to stay inside the hotel

during a No. 8. The hotels circulate a brochure telling you what to do: Close the drapes,
stay away from the windows, etc. You can stay
in your room all day reading a book, or you
can drink Singapore Slings at the bar. Or you
could do what any normal person would do:
Go shopping. If you stay indoors, you'll find
every shop in the hotel is doing a booming
business. We were even offered special typhoon prices.

Seconds Stores

We all make mistakes, so it's easy enough
to understand that Hong Kong manufacturers make mistakes as well. If a
thousand units go down an assembly
line, one of them will not be perfect enough to
pass inspection. Yet the manufacturer rarely
can afford to toss out the baby with the
bathwater. Instead, he collects all those slightly
imperfect items and sells them to a store that
doesn't mind slightly faulty merchandise.

In the industry, this merchandise is called
seconds, irregulars, or imperfects. In Hong
Kong, this merchandise is sold on the streets
or in factory-outlet stores. It's unlikely you'll
be warned that the merchandise didn't make
the grade.

Depending on the brand, the "inferior" merchandise may not have anything wrong with it.
Particularly with name goods, the quality con-
trols are so incredibly strict that when a unit
does not pass inspection, it still may *appear* to
be perfect. Possibly only the maker could find
the defect.

"Damages" almost always have something
wrong with them—but often it's fixable, or
something that doesn't upset you considering
how good the bargain is.

Here are some of the flaws that may send a unit to the seconds or damages bin; watch for them in your inspection of lower-priced name goods:

▼ a dye lot that does not match other dye lots
▼ stripes that are not printed straight or do not match at seams
▼ prints that are off-register
▼ bubbles in glass or plastic
▼ uneven finish
▼ nonmatched patterns at seams
▼ zipper set in poorly or broken zipper
▼ puckered stitching
▼ belt loops that don't match

Remember, seconds are not sale merchandise that hasn't sold; they are stepchildren. Most stores will not admit that they sell seconds. If you are shopping in a seconds resource or a factory outlet, remember to check for damages or slight imperfections. Some imperfections are more than slight.

Factory-Outlet Shopping

Since manufacturing is the business Hong Kong is in, it didn't take the business honchos long to figure out a brilliant piece of merchandising—factory outlets. Factory outlets have become so popular in Hong Kong that they are an established part of the retail structure. In fact, there are about half a dozen local publications that report on the goings-in, -out, and -on of the factory-outlet trade.

Some manufacturers have done so well in the factory-outlet business that they now produce their goods solely for their tourist and local clients—they don't even export! While most of the outlets listed in the various guides are fun to visit, many of them are rip-offs. Or, to put it more kindly, are in business just to be in business. Because it is best to shop the many outlets by neighborhood, we have an index of outlets in our Neighborhoods chapter (page 89).

The Building System

Most of us are used to finding stores on street level, with fancy glass storefronts and large numbers identifying their address. There are many such stores in Hong Kong, but many more are operated out of office buildings. You will arrive at an address to see only a cement building. Before you think that the address is wrong, go into the lobby and look at the directory. The store or business will probably be listed with a floor and room number next to it. You may think that this isn't worth the trouble, but we have found some of our best buys in shops that were the hardest to find.

Because of this practice of "office shopping," the addresses in Hong Kong usually refer to a particular building. When getting the address of a particular shop, instead of being told that it is at 17 Hankow Street, you are likely to be told that it is in the Sands Building. Luckily, many maps are marked with the actual buildings and their addresses. Cab drivers are so used to the system that you can usually give them the name of the building and they will take you right there.

If you are not using one of our tours to plan your shopping expedition, work carefully with a map so that you determine all the shops in one building at one time. Remember that it is not unusual for a business to have a shop on each side of the harbor—so decide if you are going to be in Hong Kong or Kowloon before you make plans. Use the *A-O-A Map Directory* to locate a building before you head off.

The Beijing Rule of Shopping

T he Beijing Rule of Shopping is the Asian version of our Moscow Rule of Shopping; it has nothing to do with shopping in Beijing, but does come with a twist.

Now: The average shopper, in pursuit of the ideal bargain, does not buy an item he wants on first seeing it, not being convinced that he won't find it elsewhere for less money. This is human nature. A shopper wants to see everything available, then return for the purchase of choice. This is a normal thought process, especially in Hong Kong, where every merchant seems to have exactly the same merchandise. If you live in Beijing, however, you know that you must buy something the minute you see it, because if you hesitate it will be gone. Hence the name of our international law. If you live in Hong Kong, you know the guys from Beijing can come over the hills anytime soon and take it all away. So you buy it when you can.

When you are on a trip, you probably will not have time to compare prices and then return to a certain shop. You will never be able to backtrack cities—and if you could, the item might be gone by the time you got back. What to do? The same thing they do in Beijing: Buy it when you see it, with the understanding that you may never see it again. But since you are not shopping in Beijing and you may see it again, weigh these questions carefully before you go ahead:

1. Is this a touristy type of item that I am bound to find all over town? Are there scads

of shops selling this kind of stuff, or is this something few other vendors seem to have?

2. Is this an item I can't live without, even if I am overpaying?

3. Is this a reputable shop, and can I trust what they tell me about the quality of this merchandise and the availability of such items?

4. Is the quality of this particular item so spectacular that it is unlikely it could be matched anywhere else or at this price?

The Beijing Rule of Shopping breaks down totally if you are an antiques or bric-a-brac shopper, since you never know if you can find another of an old or used item, if it would be in the same condition, or if the price would be higher or lower. It's very hard to price collectibles, so consider doing a lot of shopping for an item before you buy anything. This is easy in Hong Kong, where there are a zillion markets that sell much the same type of merchandise in the collectibles area. (This includes the entire Hollywood Road area.) At a certain point, you just have to buy what you love and not worry about the price. Understand that you always will get taken; it's just a matter of for how much.

If you are shopping for cameras, watches, or high-ticket electronics, you must go through a very elaborate bargaining process before you ever get to the price you might pay if you were going to buy. This makes comparison shopping very difficult. Vendors know how to make it even more difficult by putting the screws to you. For example, you want a camera. You have done your homework and know that the camera you want costs $275 from 47th Street Photo in New York. You decide to go to a few shops in Hong Kong to find out how the prices are running and what's available before you make the big purchase. You walk into

Shop A, which you have chosen at random, since there are several million such shops within shouting distance. The marked price on the camera is $300. You begin to bargain, because you know that $275 is the U.S. price. You finally get the price down to $250. You think this is a pretty good price, but you want to try some other shops. You thank the vendor and say you want to think about it. He says, "If you buy it right now, I'll make it $225. No one else would take this loss, but I've spent all this time with you already, and my time is valuable. If you come back later, the price will be $250." Now you are in hot water. Is this a con job to get you to commit, or must you take advantage of a great bargain when it comes your way and get on with living life? Well, we can't decide this one for you, because there are many values at stake here—which include the fun of the chase, your time, and the camera. But part of the Beijing Rule of Shopping is the understanding that a bargained price may come around only once. (On the other hand, it may come around several times. . . .) The Beijing Rule of Shopping insists that you make a deal today because the world can change by tomorrow.

Shopping Services

Hong Kong, being the shopping mecca it is, has more than its share of shopping "experts." You can ask anyone on the street "Where can I get . . . ," and you will be led to the *best* shop. Rarely will the best shops match up. Open the paper and you will see "Shopping tours of the factory outlets . . . best deals." Invariably you will be hustled to Kaiser Estates and into a jewelry manufacturer's showroom. Much referral business in

Hong Kong results in the tour operator or guide receiving a commission, from 10% to 30% of the cost of the item you are buying. The manufacturer simply tacks this on to the cost of the items he is selling. Many guided tours to the "best bargains in Hong Kong" operate on this basis.

However, there are shopping services run by expat American women that may be worth trying if you are pushed for time or overwhelmed by Hong Kong.

Temptations, for instance, is a group of expatriate American and British ladies, married to businessmen stationed in Hong Kong. They have kids, and busy lives, but shopping is their job. They are our kind of gals.

Temptations is an upfront kind of business. You pay them a flat hourly fee for their time, their connections, and their experience. They provide a limousine and lunch and take you shopping. Any commission that a shop might offer them is passed on to you. So if a merchant is offering them a 10% discount on the merchandise you pay at least 10% less for that item. They'll even step in and do some additional bargaining in order to assure you of getting the best deal possible. They are straightforward and direct, and do their best to find whatever you are looking for. In order to use their service most effectively you should be prepared to give them some ideas about your personal style and preferences, sizes, etc. They come highly recommended by a local friend who knows everything about everybody . . . sort of the Elsa Maxwell of Hong Kong.

Temptations can be booked from the U.S. or Hong Kong. It's better to book from the U.S. and to fill out their questionnaire so you can arrange a very personalized shopping tour reflecting your exact needs. Call (800) 782-9600 and ask for Lynnae Ellis. In Hong Kong, the number is listed under Temptations Asia Ltd.

Victoria's Treasures (from the U.S., call 011-852-525-6125) is very similar to Temptations, with the same price structure and elegant way of doing business.

Asian Cajun is slightly less expensive and more down-to-earth; Helen Giss (from the U.S., call 011-852-817-3687) does not consider the other two services to be her competition. She has some corporate business as well.

It's not uncommon for these shopping services to provide a newsletter free to those they have served. Sometimes the newsletters offer shopping opportunities by mail. None of these services does group tours or busloads; everything should be custom-created for your needs. Expect to pay about $200 (U.S.) for three hours of shopping with any of these organizations. Hourly rates run from $55 to $65 for each additional hour; all require a three-hour minimum booking.

Who Ya Gonna Trust?

T rust being such a desirable commodity (since it's also so elusive), the system has provided for those of us who are concerned and don't know who to trust in Hong Kong.

1. The Chinese System of Trust: The Chinese know that you can't trust anyone except family. As a result, nepotism reigns supreme. Rich people in Hong Kong (whether Anglo or Chinese) do their business within a small cadre of those they trust—most of whom are interrelated. On high-ticket items, they never take risks on outsiders or unknown vendors.

2. The HKTA System of Trust: The HKTA is the Hong Kong Tourist Association. They are a heavy-duty presence in Hong Kong and are uniformly referred to as the HKTA.

Because rip-offs are so common in Hong Kong, the HKTA put together a merchants' association. They make merchants swear to be honest when they join. In exchange, the merchants get a little red Chinese-junk sticker (it's about 6–8 inches high) to put in their window, signifying that they are approved by the HKTA and therefore honest. This is nice in theory; but let's face it, honesty can't be policed. If you have a problem, call the HKTA. They have set up a special shopper's hotline for consumers with questions or complaints. Call the main number (524-4191) and ask for the Membership Department. If the shop is not a member of the association, the HKTA will pass on the complaint to the Government's Consumer Council. If you have an inquiry, call and ask for the Shopper's Hotline. While most red-junk shops are honest, a red junk in the window is not a graven-in-stone promise that you aren't being taken. However, the HKTA does care.

3. The Lily System of Trust: We developed this one ourselves, and it is a derivation of 1 and 2. We got the skinny on a good bit of Hong Kong's retailing from a woman named Lily, who comes from one of the grand old Hong Kong British families (she's third generation Hong Kong). Lily ran off and married the son of a Chinese warlord when she was 16, and then left him when she was 25. She now lives in grand style in a villa nestled into the Peak. As a result of her background, she is related to the wealthiest of the British and the Chinese families, and knows everyone who's "in." If Lily recommends a source, it's usually trustworthy. If yet another connection in Hong Kong—from the same circle—recommends the same source, even better. Many of the stores in this book, specifically the outlets, have been recommended to us by Lily, by her friends, or by both.

Frauds and Fakes

Hong Kong has very strict laws regarding copyright violations, so outright fakes are hard to find (unlike in Korea!). Even Macao has more imitations on the street than Hong Kong. Watches are pretty easy to buy (see page 226), but Chanel-style handbags (complete with interlocking Cs) are nearly impossible to find without connections.

In some areas, like antiques, fakes are made and passed off as real to an unsuspecting buyer. Unless you have your Ph.D. in Ancient Chinese Art, you can hardly distinguish a good antique from a great fake. In this area you should only buy through a reputable dealer or auction house.

Watch Out

This is the saga of the Chanel watch we didn't buy.

Jill said she wanted a fake Chanel watch. She also specified she didn't want us to spend more than $10 for it, since she had already bought one in Hong Kong for $10.

When we were approached on Nathan Road by a young man who whispered "Get you Rolex watch, lady?" we immediately brightened.

"How about Chanel?"

"Sure."

He then asked us to follow. Apprehension set in after we ascended the second set of back staircases in a rickety poured-concrete shopping mall above Nathan Road. When the guide led us down a deserted hallway and opened the door to a broom closet filled with Chinese youths, we thought it was over. Time stopped. Who needed a watch in the Twilight Zone?

In the broom closet was a hot-water heater and three chairs, as well as five youths, one of whom had a walkie-talkie.

"Have a seat."

"No thanks."

We looked at photographs of two different Chanel-style watches; we asked to see them in person. Prices were discussed: $100 per watch. The young man with the walkie-talkie spoke into it.

Time passed. A hundred years. Maybe a thousand years. Finally the door opened: a young man walked in, his shirt stuffed with packages. The door shut behind him, and he opened his shirt to reveal five watches, including the two Chanel models we had asked to see.

The watches were almost perfect fakes, and said "Chanel" on the face, but the gold on the chain-and-"leather" strap was too yellow; $100 was out of the question. We offered $35. The door opened.

"Don't waste my time," said our host.

We were free to run. We did.

High-priced Imitations

While the market in cheap copies of designer goods seems to have dried up in Hong Kong, it is indeed the place to go to have the expensive imitations of even more expensive merchandise made for you. We like the story of our friend Mr. X (whose name we cannot tell you because it happens to be a household word). Needless to say, Mr. X's family is unreasonably wealthy. Prior to her birthday one year, Mrs. X gave her husband an ad she had torn

out of *Vogue*—she had seen a bauble from
Harry Winston that she thought would be nice.

On her birthday, Mrs. X received from her
husband the ad—stapled to an envelope containing two plane tickets to Hong Kong. The
X family flew to Hong Kong, went to Trio
Pearls, and showed them the ad. The piece
was copied for Mrs. X. Mr. X paid for the trip
and the piece of jewelry, and still saved
money.

You can get excellent reproductions of furnishings and jewelry in Hong Kong for large
savings—if you are the kind of person who
spends a lot in these categories to begin with.
You can also do well with items like furs—if
you still wear fur. No one commissions a fake
antique, but you can have a great time saving
money with fabulous "fakes" of the very real
kind. Really good fakes cost a lot and are
passed off as serious art.

Tailors also pride themselves on making copies of high-priced designs. If you want an
Ungaro original but can't pay the price, bring
the fabric and pattern to Hong Kong with you,
and a tailor will make the ensemble for you at
a fraction of the Paris price. Comparison-shop
carefully before commissioning a "designer"
outfit. Many tailors are very conservative and
will not have the kind of flair necessary to pull
off a high-fashion look. Beware the cheap-
looking Chanel-style suits, which abound. Bring
your own buttons and trims to pull off the
proper look.

Scams

Hong Kong is the original Scam City. If
you think you are street smart, you can
still learn a trick or two in Hong Kong.
If you know you are naïve, get smart now.

The wise man asks, "How can you tell if you are being cheated in Hong Kong?"

The philosopher answers, "How can you tell how much you are being cheated in Hong Kong?"

We list only shops we have done business with, and, we hope, any retail establishment listed in this book would never seriously consider cheating you. But we don't guarantee it, and it doesn't hurt to be on the ball. Markets and street vendors are much more likely to con you than established retail outlets.

▼ Feel the goods and carefully inspect any item wrapped in plastic. For example: You go to a store and see the sample silk blouse and decide to buy it. As you are paying, a seemingly identical silk blouse, perfectly wrapped in sealed plastic, is put in your shopping bag. You're no dummy, so you say, "Is that the same blouse?" You even check the size. You are assured that everything is correct and you have just been given a factory-perfect blouse that is clean—unlike the much-handled sample you chose. You smile with contentment. Fool. Open the plastic. There is a good chance that the blouse you have been given is exactly like the sample in every way—except that the silk is of an inferior quality. Feel the goods. Not everyone will cheat you. But many will try.

▼ Pick the skins for shoes or leathergoods that are being custom-made, and make it clear that you expect the skins you pick to be the skins in your garment. Have them marked with your initials. If you go for a fitting, before the linings are added, check your skins to make certain they are the same.

▼ Jade is very difficult to buy. A true test requires scientific measurement of hardness, specific density, and light refraction. Good luck, sailor. If it's not incredibly expensive and guaranteed, walk away.

▼ Never trust anyone, no matter how much you think you can trust him. Never underestimate the possibility of a scam. Murphy's Law of Hong Kong: If you can be taken, you will be.

Private Labels

Private labels are the opposite of designer labels but are now becoming competitive and exciting. Almost all big American department stores have private labels, many of which are made in Hong Kong. The private-label business is one of direct contracting.

The manufacturer who owns a license has to charge a higher price for his designer goods than his regular merchandise, because he is paying out a piece of the action to the designer. He can make that exact same merchandise and sell it without the label or the logo and charge much less. He can put his own company name in it for some product recognition and brand following, or he can sew a department-store label in it and let the store take the responsibility for convincing the public that the item is of good quality. More and more department stores are going into the private-label business, connecting their fine reputations with the quality of the merchandise they have contracted for. Familiarize yourself with U.S. department-store labels so that you can recognize these items when you see them in Hong Kong.

Shipping

We have done a good bit of shipping from Hong Kong and have good news to report: It's easy and it's safe. Container shipping is not inexpensive, but freight is moderate. Whether the item is as cumbersome as a giant Foo dog, as small as a few ginger jars, or as fragile as dinner plates, you can arrange to ship it home. All it takes is a little time and a little more money.

Remember that Hong Kong is an island and that shipping is a way of life—as it has been there for centuries. The British are used to bringing things in from overseas. People with money who live in Hong Kong automatically expect to pay the price of shipping something in—especially items of Western design. Importing is a way of life for expats; exporting is a way of life for big businesses. Shipping in and out of Hong Kong is therefore very easy.

If you anticipate buying an item that needs shipping, do your homework before you leave the United States. You may need a family member to claim the item at Customs if you will still be out of the country, or you may even need a Customs agent (see page 54). You will also want to know enough about shipping costs to be able to make a smart decision about the expense added to your purchase. To make shipping pay, the item—with the additional cost of shipping, duty, and insurance (and Customs agent, etc., if need be)—still should cost *less* than it would at home, or should be so totally unavailable at home that any price makes it a worthwhile purchase. If it's truly unavailable (and isn't an antique or a one-of-a-kind art item) at home, ask yourself why. There may be a good reason—such as that it's illegal to bring such an item into the country! If you are indeed looking for a certain type of thing, be very familiar with American prices. If it's an item of furniture, even an antique, can a decorator get it for you with a 20% rather than 40% markup? Have you checked out all the savings angles first? Are you certain the item is genuine and is worth the price of the shipping? There are many furniture fakes in Hong Kong.

There are basically two types of shipping: surface and air. Air can be broken into two categories: unaccompanied baggage and regular air freight.

Surface mail (by ship in a transpacific transaction) is the cheapest. Surface mail may mean through the regular mail channels—that is, a small package of perfume would be sent through parcel post—or it may require your filling an entire shipping container or at least paying the price of an entire container. Surface mail may take three months; we find two is the norm. If you are doing heavy-duty shipping, look in the back of the *South China Morning Post* for shippers wanting to fill containers.

If you're shipping by container but can't fill a container, you might want to save even more money by using groupage services. Your goods will be held until a shipping container is filled. The container will then go to the United States, to one of only four ports of entry (Los Angeles, New York, San Francisco, or New Orleans), where you can meet the container at the dock, be there when your items are unpacked, and then pay the duties due. A full container is approximately 1,500 cubic feet of space (or 8 feet, 6 inches by 8 feet, 6 inches by 20 feet long) and will not be delivered to your door (no matter how much you smile).

Air freight is several times more expensive than surface, but gives you the assurance of a quick delivery. We can't think of anything that would have to be flown to us in the States; if it were so delicate and so important as to need to be flown, it might indeed need an international courier, who is a person who hand-carries the item for you (often this is done with pieces of art or valuable papers). There are also overnight air package services, much like Federal Express, that deliver within a day or two. This area is growing just the way overnight U.S. services expanded in the past three years, so check out the latest possibilities. Crossing the dateline can make "overnight" deliveries seem longer or shorter.

If you want to price a few local freight offices, we have used these, or have been referred by friends who have used them with great success:

Unaccompanied Baggage Ltd.
Counter 330, Departure Hall
Hong Kong International Airport, Kowloon
769-8275

Michelle Int'l Transport Co. Ltd.
Room 1002, 20 Connaught Road West
Western District, Hong Kong
548-7617

Shop Ships and More

You can have items shipped directly from shops for you. Many Hong Kong stores, especially tailors, will ship your purchases to the United States. Most people we know who have done this are surprised when their goods arrive by UPS. Ask about the shop's shipping policies before you decide to ship—some stores will charge you for their trouble (a flat fee), then the actual shipping rate, and then an insurance fee.

Try to pay for the purchase with a credit card; that way if it never arrives you'll have an easier time getting a credit or a refund. Be

sure to ask when the store will be able to ship
the goods out. We planned to send home
some perfume so as not to have to lug it
around for a month's worth of touring. The
shopkeeper told us she was so backed up on
her shipping that it would take her at least six
weeks to mail our order. Then it would take
several weeks or months for the package to
arrive by surface mail. We took it with us.

If you want to save a little money, and if the
item is of manageable size, consider shipping
it yourself. Get the materials from a stationery
store and go to the local post office. The
Hong Kong Postal Service is amazingly efficient. Make sure you meet local requirements—
they may not allow certain kinds of tape, etc.
We suggest twine and filament packing tape.
Hand-print the labels and address the package
itself, so if they separate you still have a chance
to get the package.

The U.S. Postal Service automatically sends
all incoming foreign-mail shipments to Customs for examination. If no duty is being
charged, the package goes back to the post
office and will be delivered to you. If duty is
required, the Customs officer attaches a yellow
slip to your package, and your mail carrier will
collect the money due when the package is
delivered to you. If you feel the duty charge is
inappropriate, you may file a protest, or you
don't have to accept the package. If you don't
accept it, you have thirty days to file your
objection so the shipment can be detained
until the matter is settled.

Be sure to keep all paperwork. If you use a
freight office, keep the bill of lading. If the
shop sends your package, keep all receipts.

Ask about the policy on breakage from any
shop that ships for you.

Know the zip code where you are shipping
to in the United States.

Remember that you can ship unsolicited gifts
valued up to $50 duty-free.

We've had two contrasting experiences in

shop shipping, but both worked out fine. Our ginger jars took forever to arrive; our suits came air freight from the tailor's regular shipper in a matter of days.

Insurance

I nsurance usually is sold per package by your shipper. Do not assume that it is included in the price of delivery, because it isn't. There are several different types of insurance and deductibles, or all-risk (with no deductible); you'll have to make a personal choice based on the value of what you are shipping. Remember to include the price of the shipping when figuring the value of the item for insurance purposes. If you bought a desk for $1,000 and it costs $500 to ship it home, the value for insurance purposes is $1,500. If you have the replacement-cost type of insurance, you should probably double the price, since that is approximately what it would cost you to replace the item in the United States. If you're counting on your credit card's purchase protection plan (see page 66), remember that it only covers the replacement cost, and not the cost of shipping the item.

U.S. Customs and Duties

T o make your reentry into the United States as smooth as possible, follow these tips:

▼ Know the rules and stick to them!

▼ Don't try to smuggle anything.

▼ Be polite and cooperative (until the point when they ask you to strip, anyway. . . .)

Remember:

▼ You are currently allowed to bring in $400 worth of merchandise per person, duty-free. Before you leave the United States, verify this amount with one of the U.S. Customs offices. It is about to change, so ask your local office before you leave town. Each member of the family is entitled to the deduction; this includes infants (but not pets).

▼ You pay a flat 10% duty on the next $1,000 worth of merchandise. This is extremely simple and is worth doing. We're talking about the very small sum of $100 to make life easy—and crime-free.

▼ Duties thereafter are on a product-type basis. (Hefty levies on hand embroidery!)

▼ The head of the family can make a joint declaration for all family members. The "head of the family" need not be male. Whoever is the head of the family should take the responsibility for answering any questions the Customs officers may ask. Answer questions honestly, firmly, and politely. Have receipts ready and make sure they match the information on the landing card. Don't be forced into a story that won't wash under questioning. If you tell a little lie, you'll be labeled as a fibber and they'll tear your luggage apart.

▼ You count into your $400 per person everything you obtain while abroad—this includes toothpaste (if you bring the unfinished tube back with you), gifts, items bought in duty-free shops, gifts for others, the items that other people asked you to bring home for them, and—get this—even alterations.

▼ Have the Customs registration slips for things you already own in your wallet or easily available. If you wear a Cartier watch, for example, whether it was bought in the United States or in Europe ten years ago, should you be questioned about it, produce the registration slip. If you cannot prove that you took a foreign-made item out of the country with you, you may be forced to pay duty on it!

▼ The unsolicited gifts you mailed from abroad do not count in the $400-per-person rate. If the value of the gift is more than $50, you pay duty when the package comes into the country. Remember, it's only one unsolicited gift per person.

▼ Do not attempt to bring in any illegal food items—dairy products, meats, fruits, or vegetables. Liquor-filled chocolates are a no-no for some reason, but coffee is OK. Generally speaking, if it's alive, it's *verboten*. We don't need to tell you it's tacky to bring in drugs and narcotics.

▼ Antiques must be at least 100 years old to be duty-free. Provenance papers will help. Any bona fide work of art is duty-free whether it was painted fifty years ago or just yesterday; the artist need not be famous.

▼ Dress for success. People who look like hippies get stopped at Customs more than average folks. Women who look like a million dollars, who are dragging their fur coats, who have first-class baggage tags on their luggage, and who carry Gucci handbags, but declare they have bought nothing, are equally suspicious.

▼ The amount of cigarettes and liquor you can bring back duty-free is under government regulation. Usually, if you arrive by common carrier, you may bring in duty-free one liter of alcoholic beverages. You may bring in an additional five liters on which you must pay duty—at $10.50 per gallon on distilled spirits —so obviously you don't want to go over your allowance unless you are carrying some invaluable wine or champagne. If you drive across borders, the regulations may vary—but it's unlikely you will drive home from Hong Kong. (If you do, please write and tell all.)

You may also bring back 100 cigars and one carton of cigarettes without import duty, but there will be state and local taxes on the smokes. You cannot trade your cigar-cigarette-liquor quota against your $400 personal allowance, so that even if all you bought while abroad was ten gallons of champagne (to bathe in, no doubt), you probably will not have paid $400 but will still have to pay duty and taxes. Also please note that you must be 21 or over to get the liquor allowance, but you may be any age for the puffables—thus an infant gets the same tobacco allowance as an adult. No cigars from Cuba, please.

▼ Environmental no-nos are a big problem in Hong Kong, so U.S. Customs agents will be watching carefully.

1. Ivory cannot legally be imported into the U.S. unless it is antique and comes with papers.

2. Tortoiseshell is also forbidden, no matter where it comes from (unless, that is, it comes from a plastic tortoise).

▼ If you are planning on taking your personal computer with you (to keep track of your budget, perhaps), make sure you register it before taking it out of the country. If you buy a computer abroad, you must declare it when you come in.

3 ▼ MONEY MATTERS

Paying Up

Whether you use cash, traveler's check, or credit card, you are probably paying for your purchase in a currency different from American dollars. For the most part, we recommend using a credit card—especially in fancy stores. Plastic is easy to use, provides you with a record of your purchases (for Customs as well as for your books), and makes returns a lot easier. Creditcard companies, because they are often associated with banks, may give the best exchange rates. The price you pay, as posted in dollars, is translated on the day of your purchase. Let's say the Hong Kong dollar is trading at $7.80 to $1 (U.S.). Your hotel may only offer an exchange rate of $7.50 when you convert your money. American Express will probably give you a higher rate of exchange.

The bad news about credit cards is that you can overspend easily, and you may come home to a stack of bills. But one extra benefit of a credit card is that you often get delayed billing, so that you may have a month or two to raise some petty cash.

If possible, travel with more than one credit card. Some stores will only take MasterCard or Visa. Others will accept only American Express. Some prefer one to the other, but will accept either. Very often you can negotiate a discount for not using plastic at all.

Traveler's checks are a must—for safety's sake. Shop around a bit; compare the various companies that issue checks, and make sure your checks are insured against loss or theft. While we like and use American Express traveler's checks, they are not the only game in town. Ask around. At different times of the year, during special promotions, American Express checks may be offered free of a service charge by the banks. This is a good time to stock up. If you are a very good customer, your bank should offer this service to you, anyway. Call and ask.

Peter Chan says if you exchange money at Hong Kong and Shanghai Banking Corp. Ltd. (any branch) or Hong Seng Bank Ltd. you will get the day's rate listed in the *South China Morning Post.*

Personal Checks

We know a lot of people who travel without their checkbooks. This is very silly. Because in many places in the world (and Hong Kong is one of them), retailers are very happy to take your check. In fact, they may prefer it to a credit card.

Let's face it, Hong Kong is a place in transition. Most successful retailers (and businesspeople) have bank accounts elsewhere, so that if they have to run in 1997 they will have money secured away. Although they have banks all over the world, many like to have an American bank account. Your check will be accepted in Hong Kong, then processed through an American account.

Whether or not the people you do business with do all their banking transactions in Hong Kong is beside the point: Being able to write a check is incredibly convenient. When we make our regular pilgrimage to W. W. Chan (our tailor), we can easily order several suits. To pay for additional traveler's checks seems silly. They know this at the tailor's and take personal checks as an additional customer service.

Fluctuating Dollars

There is no question that the dollar dances, so don't let anyone tell you that the Hong Kong dollar remains constant at 7.8 to the U.S. dollar. True, it generally hovers at 7.8, but this is not a rule written in steel. If you happen to be in Hong Kong during a time when the U.S. dollar is weak and the Hong Kong stock market is going strong (as it has been recently), you may find that the official rate is 7.6 or 7.7, and that your hotel will give you no more than 7.3. Prices in this book were calculated at a flat rate of $7 (H.K.) per $1 (U.S.), according to rates prevailing at the time we did our research.

When you are shopping, it's very easy to divide prices by 8 in order to get a ballpark exchange rate between U.S. and Hong Kong dollars. But if you pay for your purchases in cash, in order to be fair to your cash flow, you must divide by the number you received in exchange—not by the bank rate. We often find it is safer to divide by 7 when the American dollar is weak.

Currency Exchange

As we've already mentioned, currency exchange rates vary tremendously. The rate announced in the paper (the *South China Morning Post*) every day is the official bank exchange rate, and does not apply to tourists. Even by trading your money at a bank, you will not get the rate of exchange that's announced in the papers.

▼ You will get a better rate of exchange for a traveler's check than for cash, because there is less paperwork involved for banks, hotels, etc.

▼ Hotels generally give the least favorable rate of exchange, but we find some flexibility here. You are limited by where you are staying, however. Many hotels will not change traveler's checks for nonpatrons. Hotel shops will often negotiate on the rate of exchange. It is important to know that day's bank rate before you start shopping. When in doubt, use your calculator to double-check.

▼ Don't change money (or a lot of it, anyway) at airport vendors, because they will have the worst rates in town. Yes, higher than your hotel.

▼ If you want to change Hong Kong dollars back to U.S. dollars when you leave, remember that you will pay a higher rate for them. You are now "buying" dollars rather than "selling" them. Therefore, never change more money than you think you will need, unless you are planning to stockpile for another trip.

▼ Have some foreign currency on hand for arrivals. After a lengthy transpacific flight, you will not want to have to stand in line at some airport booth to get your cab fare. You'll pay a very high rate of exchange and you'll be wasting your precious shopping time. Your home bank or local currency exchange office can sell you small amounts of foreign currency. No matter how much of a premium you pay for this money, the convenience will be worth it. We ask for $50 worth of currency for each country we are visiting. This will pay for the taxi to the hotel, tips, and the immediate necessities until you decide where to change the rest of your money.

▼ Keep track of what you pay for your currency. If you are going to several countries or must make several money-changing trips to the cashier, write the sums down. When you get home and wonder what you did with all the money you used to have, it will be easier to trace your cash. When you are budgeting, adjust to the rate you paid for the money, not the rate you read in the newspaper. Do not be embarrassed if you are confused by rates and various denominations. Learn as much as you can, and ask for help. Take time to count your change and understand what has been placed in your hand. The people you are dealing with already know you are a tourist, so feel satisfied that you understand each financial transaction.

▼ Determine mental comparative rates for quick price reactions. Know the conversion rate for $50 and $100 so that in an instant you can make a judgment. Then, if you're still interested in an item, slow down and figure out the accurate price. Do not make the mistake of equating Hong Kong and U.S. dollars, even as a quick mental fix. You'll be sorry later.

▼ When you check your credit-card slip before leaving the store, make sure to circle the "H.K." in front of the "$" sign. Since both currencies use the "$" symbol, you want to make very certain that your credit-card company does not bill you in U.S. dollars. When your credit-card bill arrives, double-check once again.

Bargaining as a Way of Life

When you walk into a store in New York, Paris, or London, you ask the price of an item, whip out your credit card or cash, and say "Thank you very much." No bargaining; no haggling. Not so in Hong Kong, where life is based on bargaining. Hong Kong society revolves around the art of the bargain. You want to buy an apple at the corner stand? Buy two and offer a little less than double; you will probably be successful.

Bargaining does not take place on buses, in the MTR, or in taxis (unless you are going for a long drive, or are hiring the car for a day). Hotel rooms are a flat rate. Your tailor has a flat fee. After that, you're on your own.

We must warn you that when times are tough in Hong Kong, vendors are less likely to bargain with tourists. We've fought with vendors in Stanley over $5 (H.K.) and not won out. We left a fancy store because they would not take $10 off a high-priced item.

Nowhere is bargaining more important, however, than in the various markets (see page 135). Here, it is open season on tourists and you are expected to bargain fiercely to get the best deal. Unless you come from a similar background you will very likely become exhausted and give up. Once you give up, it's guaranteed that you have just gotten the bad end of the bargain. In fierce bargaining you will know that you are getting near the fair price when the shopowner becomes less gracious and more grudgingly quiet.

If you are hoping to bargain successfully we have a few tips for you to follow:

▼ Do not try to bargain while wearing expensive jewelry or clothing. We always go to the market in jeans and a T-shirt, or old slacks and a nondescript sweater.

▼ If you are bargaining for an expensive item like a carpet, camera, or piece of jewelry, have some background knowledge. If you can find a fault with the product and emphasize that you are doing the merchant a favor by relieving him of inferior goods, you will be in a stronger bargaining position.

▼ Never chat with the shopkeeper, argue, or show that you are passionately interested in the item. The more businesslike and disinterested you appear to be, the less quickly the merchant will think that the cash is in his pocket.

▼ Always try to bargain alone. If you are with your spouse or friend, take the white hat/black hat positions. If you are the one looking at the item, have your friend talk about how he/she saw the same thing in New York and it was less money, better looking, and easier to buy.

▼ Ask to see the inside of the item (watch, camera, or electronic device). Most shopkeepers won't want to bother. If they do, look like you know what you are examining and make clucking noises as if something is wrong. If the shopkeeper says "What?" just shrug knowingly. The trick is to be on the offensive, not the defensive.

▼ Keep repeating your position and do not waver. This is a tried-and-true assertiveness-training tactic; it works. You must have a lot of time available to bargain well. Wearing down the opponent is the key to success.

▼ As a last resort in bargaining, walk away. But don't ever walk away from something you can't live without. If you're just bluffing the shopkeeper will know, and you will lose ground in the bargaining. If you are serious about walking away, the shopkeeper will more than likely offer you a final deal, with the understanding that if you do walk away the price will not go that low again. Don't be too surprised if the price the shopkeeper offers you as you start away is much lower than where the bargaining had broken off. If the item is so special that you can't live without it, pay that price. If not, then be prepared to do without. Recently we have been forced to walk, out of pride, more times than we like.

Returns, Repairs, and Rip-offs

The problem with returns, repairs, and rip-offs is that they take more time than cash to fix, and your time is what's valuable. Try not to buy merchandise abroad that you think may have to be returned. However, should you have a problem, see to it at once. Send a fax or telex rather than a letter (too slow) or phone call (no record of your complaint). Notify your credit-card company so that your bill is adjusted and the charge is held.

When you return the item, send it by registered mail to ensure that you have the signature of the person who received it. You will have to do a Customs declaration anyway, if the package is of any bulk. Let the store manager or owner know when you expect it to arrive. If the problem is serious, contact the Hong Kong Tourist Association and send them carbon copies of your correspondence. They are the authorized, government-sponsored body of the tourism industry in Hong Kong, and they have a special section set up just to deal with customer inquiries or complaints. From the U.S. call 011-852-801-7278, 9 A.M.–5 P.M., weekdays; 9 A.M.–1 P.M., Saturday. If you wish to write, the address is: Hong Kong Tourist Association, Jardine House, 1 Connaught Place, Central, Hong Kong. They will intercede on your behalf if the store is a member of their association (most are). If the store is not a member, they will pass the complaint over to the Consumer Council, a division of the city government. Hong Kong is very consumer-oriented, and does not want dissatisfied tourists. If you have a legitimate complaint, don't hesitate to pursue it.

Sometimes with better-quality merchandise you can exchange it in an American store.

This is highly unusual, since many stores are franchise operations, but it is worth a try before you start negotiating halfway around the world. If you are making a return, you must have your sales slip to prove what you paid. Don't expect a cash refund, and be happy if you get a store credit.

American outlets should repair Asian-bought European merchandise, provided it's genuine. There may or may not be a fee for this; it may be negotiable. The bigger problem is whether your "international guarantee" will be honored in the United States. Before you leave the store, check to make sure that your guarantee contains a complete description of the item, including model and serial number, plus purchase date, name and address of the shop, and official stamp. If you are buying a name-brand watch or electronic device, be sure that the store is an authorized representative. Guarantees that do not have all these items are not worth the paper they are written on. Be sure that you are not receiving a local guarantee or retailer guarantee instead of a worldwide/international guarantee. If you have been misled, first contact the head office of the store, then send your paperwork to the HKTA and your credit-card company to notify them of your dispute. You must do all of this in writing.

The last resort is, in fact, your charge card. The American Express Card offers a purchase protection plan, as do several other bankcards. Remember to save all receipts. Some plans extend the warranty of any purchase up to one extra year. Some companies ask you to sign up for the program; some plans are only for customers with "gold" cards. Check with your individual credit card company to find out the rules before you go.

Two Last Calculating Thoughts

1. Even if you have a Ph.D. in mathematics from MIT, we suggest you keep a calculator in your purse or pocket at all times. Furthermore, it should be the kind that uses batteries. Solar calculators are very cute, but your purse is dark inside, and many shops are, too. There's nothing worse than trying to do a hard bit of negotiating when your calculator won't calculate. If you use your calculator frequently, or your children like to play with it, buy new batteries before you leave on the trip.

2. The departure tax from Hong Kong is one of the steepest in the world. It must be paid in Hong Kong dollars at the time you check in at the airline counter. Credit cards, checks, and traveler's checks are not accepted. Put the money away in a safe place and don't touch it. Children have to pay too. At last notice the rate was $100 (H.K.) for adults and $150 (H.K.) for children over 12 years old. There is no departure tax for children under 12. Be sure to pay attention when you are paying the tax. An absentminded agent counted our tickets (two) and insisted on $200 (H.K.) without noticing that one of us was a child.

4 ▾ SHOPPING NEIGHBORHOODS

A Word About Neighborhoods

W hen we refer to Hong Kong in this book, we mean the island of Hong Kong. However, the whole territory includes more than Hong Kong Island —there are Kowloon, the New Territories, and many islands as well. These areas are also broken down into neighborhoods, many of which will appeal to tourists.

When people give you an address for a shop "in Hong Kong," you'll soon realize that addresses here are a combination of street, neighborhood, and city. An address like 121 Ice House Street, Central, Hong Kong, would be on Hong Kong Island, in the Central District. An address reading 6 Nathan Road, Tsim Sha Tsui, Kowloon, would be on Kowloon Peninsula, in the district of Tsim Sha Tsui.

As far as quality shopping is concerned, Hong Kong and Kowloon are the star areas. Although the New Territories are developing very quickly, and many factories are relocating there—due to land availability and cheaper rents—Hong Kong and Kowloon still contain 90% of the shops you will want to visit.

Each city is further broken down into neighborhoods, each with distinct personalities. However, due in part to the population density, people talk about neighborhoods like Central, Wanchai, Causeway Bay, and Tsim Sha Tsui as if they were cities, not neighborhoods. To find your way around, it is important to make the distinction.

Because we list shops by category in later chapters of this book, we have added a directory of listings to help you locate shops within an area. If you plan to spend the day in Central, check our index for a list of shops in that area. You'll want to plan each shopping day in Hong Kong carefully to get the most out of each neighborhood. Some people will want to just go to a neighborhood and wander, without further addresses to burden them.

Getting Around the Neighborhoods

The metro (MTR) in Hong Kong is located conveniently to most shopping areas. From one stop it is quite easy to walk to a few different neighborhoods. Use the MTR to get to the general location, then hunt down your shopping destination on foot.

NOTE: In the following sections the MTR directions are as follows: *Unless otherwise noted,* use the **CENTRAL** stop on the MTR for all Hong Kong locations; use the **TSIM SHA TSUI** stop for all Kowloon locations.

A Word About Addresses

Although we have already warned you that the address you will be given is most often the name of the building and not the street address, we want to stress that when street addresses are written out they may designate a specific door or portion of a building. So you may see different addresses for the same buildings, like The Landmark, Swire House, or Prince's Building. Don't freak out, go nuts, or assume it's an error. Simply check your trusty map. If an office building takes up a city block, as many do, the shops can claim different street addresses on all four sides! Don't panic. Once you are in the proper neighborhood, simply ask someone on the street for the right building.

The same is true when shopping the boutiques in a shopping center like The Landmark: Often the shop's address will simply be the name of the building. At other times, the address will include the shop number or other information. The easiest way to find what you're looking for is to check the directory on the main floor. Some show a schematic layout of all the shops; others, especially in the more outlet-oriented buildings, just list the names of the stores and corresponding floor numbers.

Hong Kong Island Neighborhoods

T he island of Hong Kong is very hilly, with development concentrated along the shoreline closest to Kowloon and Victoria Harbour. The central part of the island is home to many wealthy families who have secluded estates on the mountain or live in lavish apartment buildings overlooking the bay. Real estate prices here equal those in Beverly Hills or New York City. If you have a chance, take a tram to the Peak for a spectacular overview of Hong Kong.

Central

Hong Kong's financial core is located in Central. The Star Ferry terminal is located in Central. The Landmark is located in Central. Almost all of the big-name designers have their main boutiques in Central. It is the core, the hub, the banking center of Hong Kong. The Central District extends north and south from the

Hong Kong Island

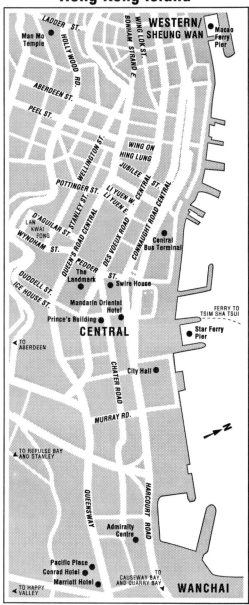

harbor to Upper Albert Road, and east and west from the Supreme Court building to just before the Macao Ferry Pier.

Shopping in Central can be glitzy or earthy. The Landmark houses five floors of shopping with stores in the basement, at street level, on a mezzanine above the street shops, and continuing up in two towers that rise above the main floors of shopping. European designers either have their shops here or across the street in Swire House, the Prince's Building, or the Mandarin Oriental Hotel. Farther west, between Queen's Road and Des Voeux Road, are the shopping lanes, Li Yuen East and Li Yuen West, where you can find good buys on purses, notions, casual clothing, and Chinese goods. If you have a strong stomach, visit Central Market, the trading area for fruit, vegetables, and meat.

Western

Western is more Chinese in flavor than any of the other Hong Kong Island neighborhoods. It was the first area to be settled by the British, who did not stay long before moving east to Central and Kowloon and leaving Western to the Chinese immigrants who came in great numbers after 1848. It has remained truly Chinese ever since.

Going west from Central, the area begins shortly after Central Market, at Possession Street, and continues to Kennedy Town, where most of the local working people live. Western includes the famous Man Wa Lane, where you can purchase your own personalized chop (see page 241), the Shun Tak Centre above the Macao Ferry Terminal, and Wing Lok Street, which is full of Chinese herbalists. The farther west you wander, the more exotic the area becomes, until you finally feel that you have left the "big" city with its towering skyscrapers and descended into traditional China. You will find "bird restaurants" where bird lovers bring their pets to have tea and compare notes, jade carvers, snake shops, handicrafts shops, and rope factories galore.

Hollywood Road

Up above Central, but within walking distance if you're wearing sensible shoes and have the feet of a mountain goat, is Hong Kong's antiques neighborhood, which is known by the name of the main drag: Hollywood Road. In the last few years, there has been some undercurrent of change as the Antiques Row in Ocean Galleries has developed further, but Hollywood Road is not passé.

Hollywood Road isn't hard to get to, but it is not necessarily on the way to anywhere else you're going. You can combine a visit here with one to the nearby Man Mo Temple for some extra cultural benefits. You can also get here from one end of the street and leave by another, so this makes a very good tour without any backtracking. But for heaven's sake, wear comfortable shoes.

If you're making this a walking tour, simply remember: up Wyndham or Pottinger; down Ladder. At the top of Wyndham Street, hang a right—Wyndham actually turns and becomes Hollywood Road. From Hollywood Road you walk along browsing the shops until you get to Cat Street (Upper Lascar Road), which is one level below Hollywood Road, and begin your descent. Not only is this the downhill stretch, but there is shopping along the way. If you are a real sport, you'll continue walking downhill toward the harbor, right into the Western District. If you wanted to see the temple, you go up before going down to Cat Street. So much for the tour. Now for what you'll actually find: antiques shops, of course.

As charming as this area is, we warn you up

front that much of what is in these shops must be considered imitation, or at least *faux*. If you are looking to do anything more serious than browse this area, we suggest you make your first stop **HONEYCHURCH ANTIQUES** (No. 29), where the expat American owners are bright, honest, and always willing to help. They know who's who and what's what in their world of dealers and will tell you about their stock and everyone else's. Glenn and Lucille Vessa are the owners; their look is an eclectic blend of antiques from around the Orient (we call it Country Chinoise); however, they know who has the more formal pieces. In fact, they know who has everything.

You can taxi to Hollywood Road and walk back down to Western, but we really want you to be a sport and walk the whole thing in order to experience one of the greatest treats in Hong Kong—getting away from the touristy world, getting away from the businesspeople in Central, and getting into a piece of exotica that will stay in your memory bank forever.

Among the better-known dealers are **IAN McLEAN** (No. 73), **ZITAN** (No. 43–55), **P. C. LU** (No. 26), **TREASURE ARTS** (No. 43), and **CAT STREET GALLERIES,** on Cat Street right below the temple. We also like **KUNG WAH LEE CHI-NAWARE COMPANY** (No. 25) and **YAU SANG CHEONG** (No. 39), who are brushmakers and stationers, **HANART** (No. 40) for Chinese paintings, and **EASTERN DREAMS** (No. 47A) for porcelains, screens, and furniture.

The most attractive of the various retail types in the quasi–flea market teeming onto the sidewalk is the entire complex at No. 47, where prices range from dirt cheap—about $3 (U.S.) for an American bestseller paperback, used but recent—to outrageous. Old postcards and photos (newly made from old plates) are sold here and make very popular souvenirs.

Many dealers sell what look like reproductions to us (although they swear this is the real stuff). **ALTFIELD** (No. 42) sells the internationally famous Jim Thompson Thai silks. The designer showroom–type shops are closer to Wyndham; the more touristy shops are near Man Mo. Our best tip is to walk down one flight of stairs at Shin Hing (an alley) and look to your left for the ceramics shop **LEE TAK CO.,** where the sign also says "Porcelain at Lowest Prices." We have to agree with the sign, and reluctantly tell you that this is one of our best resources. (Don't tell too many people.) They will only ship huge orders; and their English ain't great. This is ready-made stuff that has not been antiqued, but their blue and white has a tinge of gray in the white parts, so it doesn't look as cheap as other places'. We bought a pair of Foo dogs for the mantel for $25 (the pair).

After you've passed Man Mo there are more shops on Hollywood Road, but the real treat is to go down to Cat Street for the vendors with their wares spread on blankets and their yard-sale tactics. You can find just about anything here, from old sewing machines, hunks of jade, and Barry Manilow albums, to broken Barbie dolls and pieces of blue-and-white porcelain.

Walk down Ladder Street to Hillier Street, and into Western District and the Shuen Wan MTR station to finish off what we think you'll remember as one of the best days of shopping in Hong Kong.

Lan Kwai Fong

Although this is more of an eating neighborhood than a shopping neighborhood, its location beneath Hollywood Road and within easy walking distance of Central hotels makes it a neighborhood to know about, especially if you are a foodie or a swinger who likes your nightlife more sophisticated than in the story of Suzy Wong. This is Hong Kong's Soho, where everyone parties and goes to see and be seen. There are some boutiques in between the clubs and eateries. Weekends are a jam-packed scene, so be sure you have reservations if you plan to eat.

Wanchai

Heading east from Central, you will encounter the well-known "Suzy Wong" district of Wanchai. Back in the 1950s and 1960s this was the red-light district, frequented by sailors on leave and wealthy businessmen looking for diversion. Those days are long past, and although Wanchai's reputation lives on, all that remains are a few bars and fewer girls. Big business has slowly been encroaching and changing the face of the neighborhood. Today's most risqué nightlife comprises discos, hostess clubs, Chinese ballrooms, and topless bars.

Wanchai's latest claim to fame is the new Hong Kong Convention and Exhibition Centre (HKCEC) with its twin hotel towers. The New World Harbour View Hotel and Grand Hyatt Hong Kong Hotel have 852 and 573 rooms respectively. The complex has 18,000 square meters of exhibition space in two halls, 26 meeting rooms, and 2 theaters. Nearby are the new Arts Centre and Academy for Performing Arts. The Star Ferry provides direct access from Kowloon Peninsula as it travels from Tsim Sha Tsui to Wanchai Pier.

Old Wanchai has been pushed back from the waterfront, and will continue to be developed. If you want to see some of the original architecture and shops, prowl Queen's Road East and the lanes connecting it to Johnston Road. Shopping in the convention center is decidedly boring.

Causeway Bay

Causeway Bay, home of many hotels, offers a world of shopping and genuine Chinese sights. This area is far more funky than Central. It is bordered by Victoria Park on the east and Canal Road on the west. Its northern boundary is the harbor, while the southern is Leighton Road. Part of the bay has been filled in and is now home to the Royal Hong Kong Yacht Club. One of the most colorful parts of Causeway Bay is its typhoon shelter, where sampans and yachts moor side by side. You can have dinner on a sampan while cruising the harbor.

The main shopping in Causeway Bay centers around four Japanese department stores: **SOGO, DAIMARU, MATSUZAKAYA,** and **MITSU-KOSHI.** Behind them is one of our favorite shopping lanes, **JARDINE'S BAZAAR,** which is alive with action from early morning into the night. This is the Hong Kong we want you to see. Many of the shops in Causeway Bay stay open until 10 P.M. due to the street action. A few blocks over from the Excelsior Hotel, at right angles to Victoria Park, is Food Street, a small pedestrian mall filled with nothing but restaurants.

Causeway Bay lacks the expensive sheen of Central, but still has a lot of glitter packed in with the grime. The Excelsior Hotel—the fanciest hotel in the area—has a huge shopping arcade that most would call a mall. There are also a number of newer malls and minimalls. Most of the stores in these are designer shops, or at least sell an upscale look. Meanwhile, the local yuppies are all shopping in the Japanese department stores. In contrast to this is the street market at Jardine's Bazaar, where we once saw a bird still squawking while it was rather professionally plucked (a sight a Westerner never gets over). And in between all this (especially on Lockhart Road) are little herbalist shops selling thousand-year-old eggs and ground this and that; paper shops that sell ceremonial paper money for burning at funerals; and street vendors with donuts made of "jade."

You can get here via MTR: just get off at the Causeway Bay Station, which lets you out underneath **SOGO,** one of the best Japanese department stores. You will probably have to change trains at Admiralty (no big deal). If you come by taxi, you can get out at The Excelsior Hotel and walk through the lobby into the shopping mall. Come out the back end of the mall and work your way to Sogo, then on to Hennessy Road, where you can shop **MITSUKOSHI** and work your way toward Victoria Park, to the junction of Hennessy Road and Yee Wo Street, where **JARDINE'S BAZAAR,** an open street market, will be to your right. Wander through the food and veggie part of the market into the notions and then the souvenirs, and out behind Mitsukoshi or back out the way you came, toward Food Street and Causeway Bay or Victoria Park and its giant **ESPRIT** flagship store.

Happy Valley

Happy Valley is situated directly behind Causeway Bay and is well known for its racetrack, amusement park, and shoe shops. Horse-racing season lasts from September to June, and during this time thousands of fans stream in and out of the area. Aw Boon Haw Gardens on Tai Hang Road is Hong Kong's version of a funhouse. It is 150,000 square feet of statues set in a Chinese park that is gaudy and wild—something you will not forget.

We have heard both good and bad tales of shoe shopping in Happy Valley. Some of our Chinese friends swear by the shops along Leighton Road. We have never been too excited by them. And if you have big American feet (size

8 or larger) you shouldn't even plan on doing too much shoe shopping in Hong Kong.

Quarry Bay

With the expansion of the MTR to the end of the island and the opening of the second cross-harbor tunnel connecting Kwun Tong to Quarry Bay, shopping in North Point and Quarry Bay has begun to perk up as a real possibility for tourists.

We send you to Quarry Bay for academic reasons, with the warning that this adventure isn't for the person who is only interested in the world of luxury. This is a trip for the true traveler, who wants to see something fascinating—who understands that you only know a people by seeing how they live and how they shop.

Quarry Bay is where the Chinese yuppies live and shop. Very few tourists come out here. It has very little Old Chinese flavor, and much to remind you of American, Japanese, and British shopping traditions. Which is part of what makes this so sociologically interesting. The mansion blocks here are high-rise towers that look so much alike they are painted candy colors so you know if you live in the pink one with the fuchsia stripe or the pink one with the lavender stripe.

Amid the residential towers, there are platforms of concrete that house several malls, most notably Cityplaza II and III—we defy you to figure out what happened to I and to tell which is II and which is III. (See page 157.) They come complete with bowling, ice skating, **WHIMSEYLAND** (mechanical rides), food courts, and every store known to man.

While you can get here on the MTR (use the Taikoo Shing station, not Quarry Bay station!), this can take about forty minutes from Central. We prefer to go with a car and driver, as part of a day's outing. The drive along the harbor highway is beautiful, and you'll be fascinated by the changing scene as you drive away from Central.

Aberdeen

Say "Aberdeen" to most tourists and they think of the floating restaurants this waterside community is famous for. Say "Aberdeen" to us and we think pottery and porcelain. While the community is a bit out of the way, for those staying long enough to relax and go for the gold, it's a place to see some colorful sights and yes, do a little shopping. Ocean Park is at the edge of Aberdeen (if you have the kids with you), but it doesn't compare to Typhoon Lagoon, so beware. Aberdeen is halfway to Stanley, and you can easily combine the two as a day trip.

Get to Aberdeen on the No. 7 or No. 70 bus from the Central Terminal; the price is $2 (H.K.)—about a quarter! We prefer the No. 7 bus because you'll have no trouble getting off at the right place: Aberdeen Centre. Aberdeen Centre is easily recognized by its housing towers and bustling crowds. From here you can walk to the water for a meal at one of the three famous floating restaurants, or catch a boat to Lamma Island, or enjoy a private sampan ride. Across the street away from the water is the **ABBA SHOPPING CENTRE.** When you've finished with all this area offers, walk two blocks west to Aberdeen's Old Main Street. Then comes the serious part of the day. Send the husband and kids off in their own taxi to play at Ocean Park while you hop a taxi for china (not China). Dash to **WAH TUNG CHINA CO.** in a taxi, but plan on needing a truck to get home—this is the place for pottery. There's some 30,000 square feet of breakables here. They claim to have the largest selection in the world, and they ship (see page 247). Hours are 9:30 A.M. to 5:30 P.M. Monday through Saturday,

and 11 A.M. to 5 P.M. on Sunday. This happens
to be a great Sunday adventure, by the way.
You can even call Wah Tung and they'll come
and fetch you: 873-2272. This is a fabulous
way to shop. The showroom is in a warehouse;
follow the signs to the elevator. There are four
floors of glorious finds. Don't mind the price
tags; negotiate for a 30%–40% discount.

Stanley/Repulse Bay/Ocean Park

Not only is Stanley Market worth visiting for
shopping (see page 137), there's luxury shopping in the Repulse Bay minimall. We think
it's worth the trip to "the other side of the
island" to see the most beautiful part of Hong
Kong Island. Repulse Bay is developing as one
of the major recreation and beach areas of the
island, with new hotels and expanded facilities. It is exceedingly crowded on the weekends, but delightfully quiet midweek. You can
visit Stanley village, shop, and get in a little
time at the beach all in one easy trip.

Ocean Park, opened in 1977, is back across
the island, toward Aberdeen, halfway between
Central and Stanley. There are two parts, low-
land and highland, connected by a cable-car
ride. The amusement park section, Water
World, opened in 1984, boasts the longest
roller coaster in the world. You can easily
spend a day or more shopping and sightseeing
in this part of Hong Kong, especially if you
have kids with you. Souvenir T-shirts are
available.

Kowloon Peninsula

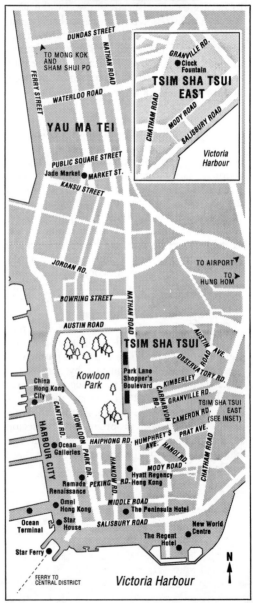

Kowloon Neighborhoods

T he peninsula of Kowloon was ceded to the British during the Opium Wars, in one of three treaties that created the Royal Crown Colony of Hong Kong. We think it was the best gift Britain ever received.

Kowloon is packed with shops, hotels, excitement, and bargains. You can shop its more than four square miles for days and still feel that you haven't even made a dent.

Like Hong Kong Island, Kowloon is the sum of many distinct neighborhoods.

Tsim Sha Tsui

The tip of Kowloon Peninsula is made up of two neighborhoods: Tsim Sha Tsui and Tsim Sha Tsui East. It is home to most of the fine hotels, and the heart of serious shopping in Kowloon. At the very tip of Tsim Sha Tsui are the Star Ferry Terminal and the Harbour City Complex. This western harborfront includes Ocean Terminal, Ocean Galleries, Ocean Centre, the Omni Marco Polo Hotel, Omni The Hong Kong Hotel, and the Omni Prince Hotel. It has miles and miles of enclosed shopping with no sight of sky. Jules Verne would have loved it.

Tsim Sha Tsui is also home to the famous Peninsula Hotel, Regent Hotel, and Ramada Renaissance Hotel. The heart of Tsim Sha Tsui, however, is Nathan Road, Kowloon's main shopping drag. Nathan Road stretches from the waterfront for quite some distance and works its way into the "real people" part of Kowloon in no time at all. The most concentrated tourist shopping is in the area called the Golden Mile, which begins on Nathan Road where it runs perpendicularly from Salisbury

Road. Both sides of this busy street are jam-packed with stores, arcades, covered alleys, and street vendors. There are also some hotels here, each with a shopping mall. If you are walking north (away from the harbor), you'll pass the Golden Mile as you get to the mosque on your left-hand side and then the Park Lane Shopper's Arcade, also on the left. To your right, across the street from Park Lane, is Burlington Arcade. The next street on your right is Granville Road, which is famous for its outlet stores. Although there are no sure-fire buys, it's still fun to wander here and get deeper into the "real people" shopping and away from the tourist push. Few tourists wander to Granville Road, which is their loss, because if you hit it big here, you'll find name-brand U.S. goods in the $10-per-item range. (Most take the MTR to venture farther north.)

While Nathan Road is the core of Kowloon, our favorite part of Tsim Sha Tsui is actually a bit off the beaten path, although directly in sight. In the Golden Mile section of Tsim Sha Tsui, there are two streets that run parallel to Nathan Road and are centered between the Golden Mile and Ocean Terminal: Lock Road and Hankow Road. They are essentially right behind The Peninsula Hotel.

If you have adventure in your soul, we ask you to wander this area with your eyes open. It's crammed with shops and neon signs and construction and busy people, and does not get so many tourists because it has the aura of being hidden. At the top of Lock Road, right before you get to Haiphong Road, look to your left, where you'll find a small alley that leads all the way through to Hankow Road. This is called the Haiphong Alley, and it is crammed with vendors. Many of these vendors do not speak English, and will drive a very hard bargain, if they bargain at all. Who cares?

Harbour City

Although technically still part of Tsim Sha Tsui, the western portion of Kowloon we call Harbour City includes more than just the Ocean Terminal shopping complex. To us, the entire stretch of Canton Road from the Star Ferry to China Hong Kong City is Harbour City, and the buildings across the street on Canton Road, like Silvercord and the Sun Plaza Arcade, are also in this same neighborhood. Perhaps it would be fairer to call this neighborhood Canton Road, but the truth is, the buildings are almost indistinguishable from each other, many are joined together, and after half a day's shopping you may be hard pressed to name which one you are in or even which side of the street you are on! It's all one big Harbour City to us, and we invite you to share our philosophy.

Also note that if you are arriving from the Hong Kong side, it's easier to get to this part of Tsim Sha Tsui by the Star Ferry. You'll be right there when you land. If you take the MTR, you'll have to walk two blocks.

The denser shopping is on the Ocean Terminal side, where (walking away from the Star Ferry) the buildings, in order, are: Star House, Ocean Terminal, Ocean Galleries, Ocean Centre, World Financial Centre, Omni Prince Hotel, and China Hong Kong City, which is a mall-and-towers complex and ferry terminal. This entire stretch of shopping buildings also includes office space and residential towers, as well as some of the well-known tourist hotels in this area, the Omni Marco Polo, Omni The Hong Kong Hotel, and the Omni Prince. Confusing? Not really. Just consider the whole thing Harbour City.

On the right-hand side of Canton Road, beginning at Peking Road, there's the Sun Plaza

Arcade and then the Silvercord Building. Silvercord has probably the best **CHINESE ARTS & CRAFTS** branch, a **LACE LANE,** and computers. Sun Plaza has a few big names (**IKEA, MITSUKOSHI**), but is not really a good mall, especially for tourists. Most of the stores cater to local yuppies and have European-style home furnishings.

If possible, avoid this entire area on weekends (especially in summer), when locals come not only to shop but to enjoy the air-conditioning. It is crowded!

Tsim Sha Tsui East

If you have Hong Kong Harbour to your back, Ocean Terminal to your left, and the Regent to your right, you are looking at the heart of Kowloon or Tsim Sha Tsui. As the Kowloon Peninsula curves around the harbor and land juts away from Kowloon and the Regent, the area just east of Tsim Sha Tsui but before Hung Hom and the airport is known as Tsim Sha Tsui East. Because it is waterfront property, it has become known mostly for its string of luxury hotels. And where there are luxury hotels, you know there are shopping opportunities.

Although the MTR does not come over in this direction, the walk to Tsim Sha Tsui station is not unreasonable—even in the noonday sun. The hotels here are anchored by the Shangri-La and the Nikko, directly overlooking the harbor, with the Regal Meridien and a few others right behind them, offering water views from some of the higher floors. The waterfront street continues as Salisbury Road, and you are essentially just down the street from the Peninsula and the Regent. The street between the two rows of hotels is Mody Road, also a main shopping street in this unusual neighborhood.

Tsim Sha Tsui East strikes us as an older version of Taikoo Shing: It is a city unto itself and is mobbed on weekends by local shoppers. Tsim Sha Tsui East is separated from Tsim Sha Tsui by a greenbelt of park complete with an elaborate fountain right behind Auto Plaza (where there's an **ESPRIT** branch). The various buildings include Auto Plaza, Houston Centre, and of course the enclosed mall itself, which is Tsim Sha Tsui Centre (see page 158). There is street-level shopping all along Mody Road, in the various buildings, inside the mall itself (of course), and then on street levels of the buildings that lead over to the side, behind the Nikko. There is even a branch of **WHIMSEY-LAND,** a kiddie park with small rides and entertainments. In ChinaChem, right behind the Nikko, there's a **DFS** store. There is also some shopping inside each of the hotels.

Yau Ma Tei

Above Tsim Sha Tsui, if you go north on Nathan Road or Canton Road, is the district of Yau Ma Tei, small and easily overlooked—unless you are in town on a boat during a typhoon, in which case you will want to know about the large typhoon shelter, which houses a community of boat people similar to the one in Aberdeen. The most famous shopping site in the area is the well-known Jade Market at Kansu and Battery streets. Here you can shop from 10 A.M. until 4 P.M. (although many shops close about 2:30 P.M.), going from stall to stall negotiating for all the jade that you might fancy (see page 140).

At night you will want to visit the Temple Street Market. As you push your way through the shoulder-to-shoulder crowds you'll have the chance to buy from the carts, have your fortune told, or enjoy an open-air meal. (See page 140.)

Hung Hom/Kwun Tong/
Sham Shui Po/Mong Kok

You say you want to get down and dirty with the real people, see some of the quickly vanishing world of yesteryear, get into a few factories for good shopping, and see someone skin a live snake and swallow its gall bladder? Step this way, folks.

HUNG HOM: Don't say ho hum to Hung Hom, because this area has really cleaned up its act. It is better described by individual factory outlets (this area is fast becoming Westernized and even touristy; see page 98), although there are also "real people" parts where few tourists explore.

KWUN TONG: Home to the less fancy factory outlets whose addresses and directions you can find in any local shopping guide, this area takes a while to travel to, and you'll get lost frequently, but it is genuine. With Leather Concepts now located in Central, there's not as much reason (to us) to even go to Kwun Tong, but we do recommend it to those who crave adventures in the real world.

SHAM SHUI PO: For more adventures of a very real kind, hit the food markets in the streets just down from the Sham Shui Po MTR station, where Kwelin Street crosses Ki Lung Street. You can walk around the city block to see live fish wriggling in red plastic bins, heaps of bok choy, and cages of bound bamboo sheltering fowl of every type. Watch more carefully to see the true details of market life. This is not for young children or the squeamish.

Sham Shui Po is also headquarters to the wholesale computer world, where video games can be bargained for and will cost anywhere from 25% to 75% less than U.S. prices. Head for **GOLDEN ARCADE SHOPPING CENTRE,** at 44B Fuk Wah Street: you'll see it from the MTR station.

MONG KOK: This area is clustered around Upper Nathan Road, where the tourists thin out and the real people shop. The Mong Kok Market is a night market of much interest to locals but with nothing that impresses us.

Factory Outlets by Neighborhood

The words "factory outlet" are music to the ear of any true shopper. Once the ultimate fantasy of the tourist visiting Hong Kong, factory outlets have now become an integral part of the shopping scene. There are, in fact, hundreds of factory outlets in Hong Kong. It is a trend in Hong Kong's manufacturing business to have your own. They are located in nice neighborhoods, out-of-the-way neighborhoods, scary neighborhoods, and chic neighborhoods. Finding all of them is easy; getting to all of them in a short amount of time (three days) is impossible. But don't panic; many of them are not worth getting to.

Each year more and more factory owners have gotten wise to the fact that the tourist wants a bargain, wants to buy at a factory, and is disappointed when she cannot do so. Some of them advertise in the *South China Morning Post* and in the tourist handouts that are provided at the airport by the HKTA. Many of them actually belong to the Hong Kong Tourist Association and have received their approval and sticker. The outlets in Kaiser Estates have made shopping easy by banding together and forming an association. The result of all this activity has been to generate mass "factory-mania" in the industry. Some of the most commercial outlets have let their merchandise become shoddy and second-rate. The real bargains have disappeared and been replaced by manufactured bargains. Factories that are new to the game are competing hard for the business. Many have opened beautiful, clean "outlets" staffed with English-speaking sales help. The merchandise is as good as you would get in a boutique—definitely not seconds. We don't complain too much as long as the bargain is still there and the price is right. In many cases this is not true. High rents mean higher prices. Don't expect to find a great deal in a factory-outlet shop that has a tony address.

The famous designer labels that you might hope to find in the outlets have put restrictions on their factories because of the serious problem of rip-offs that has plagued them in the last few years. Current merchandise has been known to "disappear" from the factory and reappear under a different label at a factory outlet. Sometimes the style is slightly modified; sometimes it is not even changed. Many factories that you would hope to visit are closed and guarded.

Having learned and relearned it all the hard way (hours on the MTR in search of a bargain and winding up with junk; wearing through many pairs of Reeboks walking the back alleys of Kowloon and the New Territories), we are here to keep you from making the same mistakes we made. We have revisited, edited, added, and listed only those outlets that we think are worth visiting. If we have left some out, it is either because they are inaccessible or because the quality of the merchandise was not up to our standards. If you have only three to five days in Hong Kong, you don't have time to waste. Be sure that you are not planning your factory-outlet visits on a public holiday, and especially not during the Chinese New Year, when everything will be closed up tight. Remember that factories and their outlets close during lunch, usually from 1 P.M. to 2 P.M. Remember, there is a local guide to outlets only, if you crave more (see page 15).

Ambience in the outlets varies widely. Some good outlets are in the factories themselves, and are exciting to visit. Other outlets are funky but have good-quality merchandise mixed in with seconds. More and more of our favorite outlets are quite elegant, have large, modern showrooms, and accept credit cards; nevertheless, they offer quality merchandise at discount prices. One thing to remember about shopping in an outlet is that there are no returns or credits. Once you leave the store, the merchandise is yours, even if you find a huge hole in the sleeve when you return to your hotel room. Always check the merchandise for dye lots and damages before you buy it. Always try on an item; verify sizes. Most outlets will have some place for you to try on items. Sizes are not always marked correctly. As with the rest of Hong Kong shopping, the motto is "Buyer Beware." When possible, shop with a credit card that has an automatic purchase protection plan so you can get a refund in case of disaster.

One note of warning: In Hong Kong, stores seem to move about faster than the prevailing winds. Despite our best efforts to keep this book current, a few stores will, no doubt, fall between the publication of one edition and the next. If a store is no longer at the address we have listed, we apologize. We no longer list the specific designer names carried by the outlets, unless they themselves advertise it, for the exact same reason. Designers jump from one manufacturer to the next at a moment's notice, leaving the once great outlet high and dry. If the outlet is particularly out of your way, you might want to double-check that it is still there. Remember, this is Hong Kong ... expect anything.

Central

Central is the main retail shopping, banking, and business hub of Hong Kong. The rents are very high. Get the message? Because more and more tourists are looking for factory outlets that are convenient, more and more manufacturers are complying by opening branches in Central. However, you cannot expect to get a fabulous bargain in a shop where the overhead is outrageous. We recommend shopping the Central outlets for fun and convenience. It sure beats an hour on the MTR and getting lost in Kwun Tong. But you will pay the price for this convenience. For many, time is money. Unless we have specifically noted, these outlets all accept some form of credit card, usually MasterCard, Visa, and/or American Express.

BETU: Betu, located in the Pedder Building, is only for the strong. Nevertheless, Betu carries private-label merchandise that is better priced than what you find in the department stores. There are no fabulous designer-label "deals," but the shop is clean and convenient, and the merchandise is well organized. The bigger, better Betu is in Kwun Tong (at 203 Wai Yip Street), but that is a trip you wouldn't want to take just for this. Hours here are Monday–Saturday, 9:30 A.M. to 6:30 P.M.

BETU, Pedder Building, 12 Pedder Street, Hong Kong

▼

CAMBERLEY: This is the easiest Camberley location to find, although there is another one in Kowloon. They manufacture for top designers, and we have seen clothing from two big-name designers hanging on the racks. Camberley's quality surpasses that at most factory-outlet shops. We like their silk blouses under $100 and their suits in gabardine or silk/linen blends for under $200. A famous-name designer's silk dresses were selling for $100. The shop is located upstairs in Swire House. Hours are Monday–Saturday, 9 A.M. to 6 P.M.

CAMBERLEY, Swire House, Connaught Road Central, Hong Kong

▼

ÇA VA: One of the "office building" outlets in Central, Ça Va carries export merchandise, not seconds. They do not claim to be a true factory outlet, and are straightforward about the fact that they sell the Marisa Christina and Ciao Sports lines in the shop. During the January–February and June–July–August sale periods, they dispose of all the factory samples through their three outlets. This is the time to come and save money. Ça Va manufactures a full line of clothing, mostly in silks and gabardines. Prices are midrange, with a suit costing $250 and silk blouses $100. Ça Va is open Monday–Friday from 10:30 A.M. to 6 P.M., and Saturday from 10:30 A.M. to 5 P.M.

ÇA VA, Central Building, 19–23 Queen's Road Central, Hong Kong

▼

JENNIE: It's in a new location, but Jennie's rep is intact. Actually, this is near their original Quarry Bay headquarters, just reopened in a new spot. The merchandise includes sweaters, silk blouses, pleated silk skirts, gabardine blazers, and cotton knits of all varieties. The average price of anything is $50. The outlet is crowded with Hong Kong locals. There are no labels that we recognize, and the merchandise looks like upscale private-label to us. Hours are Monday–Saturday, 10 A.M. to 7 P.M. No credit cards.

JENNIE, Melbourne Industrial Building (17th floor), 16 Wetlands Road, Hong Kong (MTR: Quarry Bay)

SHIRT STOP: This outlet has become so popular that it has multiplied and spawned many others around town. We shop in Kowloon because it's convenient. Shirt Stop specializes in men's shirts, most especially from a major French designer with three initials. They are very up front about displaying the merchandise, labels intact and all. Other designer goods have labels cut, but it is still possible to read them. Much of the merchandise is unisex. There can be items other than shirts and sweaters; we lucked into gorgeous terry robes on our last trip. Shirt Stop is a good place to stock up on everyday shirts at good prices. A button-down cotton runs $20 or less. There are also sweaters in wool and cashmere for sale. The heavy knits are less expensive and a better value than the cashmeres.

SHIRT STOP, Hyatt Regency Hotel Arcade (Basement), 67 Nathan Road, Kowloon

▼

SHOPPER'S WORLD SAFARI: This is what a factory outlet should look like. It was one of the first, and may be one of the last. It is dingy, crowded, and packed with people and merchandise. You have to be Inspector Clouseau to find the designer goods here, but they are here. Much of the merchandise looks like it has been around since the store opened. We don't think it has been; it is just factory rejects, seconds, or damages. Over the years we have found major big-name designer goods in the racks. You will either luck out or be sorry you bothered. The seasons make a big difference. Other shops are located in Kowloon, at the Sands Building, 17 Hankow Road, and at Jade Mansion, 40 Waterloo Road. Hours at the Pedder Building are Monday–Sunday, 9:30 A.M. to 6:30 P.M.

SHOPPER'S WORLD SAFARI, Pedder Building, 12 Pedder Street, Hong Kong

TAKPAC: A smart, modern outlet in the Pedder Building that features Anne Klein II; but we say "Yawn." There are lots of choices to make in lots of colors. We don't know where the merchandise is sold retail, however, because it is not typical U.S. goods. A lot of the clothing is small. A lot looks old. Prices are no better than at a good sale in the United States. Look in and see if you find anything. Chantal Thomas clothing is also sold. The location certainly is convenient. Hours are Monday–Saturday, 9:30 A.M. to 6:30 P.M.

TAKPAC, Pedder Building, 12 Pedder Street, Hong Kong

▼

WINTEX: One of the tonier outlets in Central, Wintex carries the Lisa Ferranti and Vanessa Van Cleef labels. All the clothing is spanking clean; much of it is still in plastic. Prices average around $100–$200 for a blouse, which we don't consider to be much of a bargain. They advertise "wholesale prices," but we don't think these goods would retail for double what you will pay here. You can put together a complete outfit and not worry about holes, however. We paid $130 for a cashmere sweater. Hours are Monday–Friday, 9 A.M. to 6 P.M., and Saturday till 5 P.M.

WINTEX, Pedder Building, 12 Pedder Street, Hong Kong

Tsim Sha Tsui

Tsim Sha Tsui and Tsim Sha Tsui East are the focal areas where Kowloon Peninsula's "retail" outlet shops have located. These outlets, usually found in commercial buildings, cater to the tourist trade, while still trying to pass on a bargain or two. We must warn you that looking for an address is frustrating, however. Many buildings are old, and their numbers have been worn away or buried under shop signs. In our listings, we give building names for this reason. The name of any building seems to be more clearly marked than the street address is. Travel with the *A-O-A Map Directory*. You can match up buildings by name and location in the block to find the right doorway. We give as specific directions as possible, but even we still get lost. Credit cards are accepted at these shops unless so noted. You can take the MTR to the Tsim Sha Tsui stop for the following stores, unless otherwise noted.

SANDS BUILDING
17 Hankow Road, Kowloon

The Sands Building is not a factory-outlet building, although you might think so from all the listings. It is an office building, located right in the heart of the action, next door to the Chung Kiu Department Store. (Don't miss Chung Kiu, if you like Chinese department stores.) The entrance to the Sands Building is to the right of the store. Go to the back to find the elevators to the shops:

ORIENTAL PACIFIC, 6th floor: O.P. is an old hand at the outlet business, and we are glad they still have good prices. We could ramble on for hours about the bargains we have found here, the sweaters we are still wearing, the single- and double-ply cashmeres that are unbeatable for design and price. O.P. is a real find. The shop is quite large, with sweater bins and racks lining three of the four walls. Displays are arranged by quality. Summer cottons are in one area, children's clothing in another, cashmeres on the wall nearest to the cash register. Sizes all tend to be marked large, but there is stock in the back; just ask. If a salesperson tells you that is all they have, ask the manager. Trust us, the back room has boxes upon boxes of sweaters.

Some of the sweaters may appear worn or old at first glance. Examine them carefully and you'll probably see that it's a combination of the lighting, the wool, and the colors. We stock up on kids' wool sweaters. They are not, we repeat not, designer sweaters. If you expect glamorous styles here you will be disappointed. These are basics. These are bargains. Oriental Pacific in Star House (6th floor, Canton Road) is a prettier, fresher, and newer store. The stock is all the same. Expect to pay $150–$200 for a cashmere pullover. We think the best buys are the men's heavy woolen sweaters. Hours in both stores are Monday–Saturday, 9 A.M. to 6 P.M.

TOP KNITTERS, 10th floor: Top Knitters produces knitwear for some of the major, major, major designers. If you are up on designs, you will recognize them. This is one of those feast-or-famine outlets; we wish you good hunting. Don't expect cheap. Hours are Monday–Friday, 9 A.M. to 6 P.M., Saturday till 5 P.M.

DORFIT, 11th floor: Dorfit is a small version of Oriental Pacific. There are sweaters piled all over the room. Some are a little seedy, but if you ignore these and concentrate on the cashmeres and cottons, you will love it here too. A good two-ply cashmere man's or woman's pullover should run no more than $200. Dorfit also carries a fun and inexpensive line of children's sweaters. There are two other shops in Kowloon, at 23–25 Nathan Road and in Harbour City/Ocean Centre, 5 Canton Road.

Granville Road

We can sum up Granville Road shopping by simply telling you that we had $50 left in Hong Kong money and one hour before checking out of the Regent, so we strolled along Granville Road and returned home with enough bags to fill a suitcase, and still had enough money to tip the bellman!

We have been on Granville Road when bargains are dried up and when they are flowing; when it's good, this is as close to shopping heaven as you will get. We're not going to name stores, but you don't need names. Just start at the McDonald's one block into Granville Road from Nathan Road and walk east until the street ends. Please note that these stores do not take credit cards. Many will take U.S. dollars but will peg the rate of exchange where they want it—which may be better than you'll get at your hotel, anyway. There is one place to change money toward the end of the stretch across from the Ramada. Bring cash and maybe a trailer. The last time we were there labels from The Gap, The Limited, Victoria's Secret, Harvé Benard, Mexx, Eddie Bauer, Banana Republic, and Calvin Klein were all hanging around.

Just go from store to store; don't worry about names and addresses. Or hit **VALUE** (No. 32), **SAMPLE NOOK** (No. 30), **GX WAREHOUSE** (No. 26), **FACTOR FASHION CO.** (No. 26A), and **STOCK SHOP** (No. 32A).

Hung Hom

Once you are out of Tsim Sha Tsui, you have entered the world of true factory outlets. Hung Hom is the neighborhood closest to Tsim Sha Tsui, and was the first to make factory-outlet shopping an event. Kaiser Estates Phase I, II, and III are the mainstays of Hung Hom, although there are three other buildings where outlets have popped up as well.

Getting to Hung Hom is best done in a taxi. We hate to give in to convenience, but if you have never been there before, it really is the smart way to go. The taxi ride costs $40

(H.K.). Ask to be let out in front of Kaiser Estates Phase I, as the majority of the shops are located either in Kaiser Estates or in the Winner Building across the street. If you are compelled to come by bus, routes 5C, 8, and 25 leave from the Kowloon Star Ferry Terminal. Get off at Ma Tau Wei Road, just after Station Lane. Walk to Man Yue Street for Kaiser Estates. To return, backtrack and catch the bus on the other side of Ma Tau Wei Road marked "Star Ferry." Taxis come and go on a regular basis in front of Kaiser Estates Phase I. Better yet, consider coming with a car and driver if you want to check out the scene and then move on.

ÇA VA: We don't want you to miss this branch of Ça Va, if you didn't visit it in Central. Ça Va is well known for silks. You can buy shirts, still in the plastic wrap, for under $50. The styles are not exciting, but we are happy wearing them under suits. Marisa Christina sweaters are also featured. If you come at the right time of year, there is a good selection. Sample sale times are January–February, June, and July–August. You will get your best buys then. Hours are Monday–Friday, 10:30 A.M. to 6 P.M., Saturday to 5 P.M.

ÇA VA, 34 Man Yue Street (ground floor), Kowloon

▼

VICA MODA: Vica Moda is across the street from Phase I and is known for its casual coordinates. We fell in love with a silk-and-cashmere sweater here that was $200 worth of scrumptious. There were also washable silk pants for $40, and silk shells for $20–$40. Hours are Monday–Saturday, 9:30 A.M. to 6:30 P.M.

VICA MODA, Winner Building, 32 Man Yue Street, Kowloon

JOSEPH HO: If you've checked out Joseph Ho's line in any of the retail boutiques and like it, then don't miss his outlet, which is as fancy as any mall shop.

JOSEPH HO, Winner Building (1st floor), 36 Man Yue Street, Kowloon

▼

FOUR SEASONS GARMENTS: We would say "Don't waste your time," but you won't listen, so go and look. Four Seasons was one of the first factory outlets to open its doors to the public. There is a factory. However, success has gone to their heads and now the outlet is run purely for profit from the tourist. Few locals shop here. We do like the items made just for gifts, such as the Chinese silk happy coats for $50, or the packaged and labeled silk shells for $8. Regular silk blouses are now $50 and up. The shop is located in Phase II, at the top of the escalators to the left. Hours are Monday–Saturday, 9 A.M. to 6 P.M.

FOUR SEASONS GARMENTS, Kaiser Estates Phase II (1st floor), 51 Man Yue Street, Kowloon

▼

LIM YING YING: We have followed this line from small crowded shop to small crowded shop. All of our favorite lingerie designers are hanging on the racks. Granted there's not a big selection of all designs in every size, as you would find in Neiman Marcus. But if you luck out, you really luck out. We found a big-name designer robe for under $50 on our last visit. It would have retailed for triple that at Neiman's. There are a lot of Joseph Ho look-alikes and midrange cotton sweaters as well. Don't forget to check the silk lingerie for damages. Remember, that's how it got to be so cheap! The Hang Fung Industrial Building is across the street from Kaiser Estates Phase III. Enter on Hok Yuen Street, which intersects Man Yue Street after it turns the corner. Lim Ying Ying is on the 1st floor. This building is very industrial and may frighten you. The elevator is not automatic; sometimes you might have to run it yourself. Hours are Monday–Saturday, 9:30 A.M. to 6 P.M.

LIM YING YING, Hang Fung Industrial Building (1st floor), 2G Hok Yuen Street, Kowloon

▼

FASHIONS OF SEVENTH AVENUE: This is a hot source for locals, who claim they get very big-name stuff here. The racks are cleaned out as quickly as the merchandise comes in. Fashions of Seventh Avenue is located in the most out-of-the-way part of Kaiser Estates, in Phase III. As you exit the elevator on the 9th floor, look for an office marked "M." The outlet is inside. The boutique is simple and spare. There are lots of good-quality silk bodysuits and knits hanging along the perimeter; suits and separates fill racks. Sizes are strange and prices are high. There are no labels. There is also an outlet in Central (8 Queen's Road Central). There was no crossover in merchandise between these two stores when we visited. Hours are Monday–Saturday, 9 A.M. to 6 P.M. Phase III is around the corner from Phase I. There is another shop at Convention Plaza, 11 Harbour Road, in Central (MTR: Wanchai).

FASHIONS OF SEVENTH AVENUE, Kaiser Estates Phase III (9th floor), Hok Yuen Street, Kowloon

▼

EDE: Even though we're not sure how to pronounce this name, we can tell you how to pronounce the goodies: swell. This medium-sized outlet has moderately priced suits and women's clothing with some separates. We bought a Ralph Lauren Polo long-sleeved cream-colored silk blouse for $45 with label intact; an Ellen Tracy short-sleeved silk blouse was also $45. That doesn't mean these same deals will be available when you stop by, and don't tell anyone we named names. Just remember that we were thrilled with the resource and can't wait to go back. Hours are Monday–Saturday, 9:30 A.M. to 6:30 P.M.; closed Sunday.

EDE, Kaiser Estates Phase I (1st floor), 41 Man Yue Street, Kowloon

▼

DIANE FREIS FACTORY OUTLET STORE: Diane Freis no longer sells from her factory in the boonies—luckily for us, since this convenient, clean, spacious outlet is on your regular everyday shopping route. We promise that your heart will stop when you see all the choices. Most of the clothes are on racks organized by style and price. There are some bins, and there is a dress-up area with hats and some accessories. This is one of the largest outlet stores in Kaiser Estates; it takes credit cards. Dresses are in the $100–$200 range; some of them are more than a year old—but that's the beauty of a Diane dress: No one can tell.

DIANE FREIS FACTORY OUTLET STORE, Kaiser Estates Phase 1 (10th floor), 41 Man Yue Street, Kowloon

Lai Chi Kok

Now we are talking factory town. Lai Chi Kok is midway on a factory tour between Kowloon and Kwun Tong. It is safe, the MTR access is great, and all of these outlets are within walking distance. You are in a real factory town, even though it's one of the nicest, so expect to get lost and become frustrated, confused, and anxious as you search for that elusive bargain. But trust us, the bargains are out there waiting. Get out your courage and forge ahead.

Getting to Lai Chi Kok is the easy part. From Central or Tsim Sha Tsui station, get on the train marked "Tsuen Wan." Stay toward the front of the train to be near the right exit at Lai Chi Kok station. Follow the signs for Leighton Textile Building and Tung Chau West Street. When you reach the street, walk ahead and cross Tung Chau West to locate Splendid. *Note:* When crossing back and forth on Cheung Sha Wan Road and Tung Chau Road, don't be too brave, or foolish. The traffic is terrible. Use the lights to cross.

SPLENDID: Once you find the 916 address, walk back to the garage and then to the rear, where you will find the elevators, marked "lifts." Splendid is located on the 7th floor, behind gray doors, in a large showroom attached to the factory. It looks too modern and clean to have good bargains, but don't let the nice appearance stop you. Splendid manufactures upscale leather clothing for European stores. Many lines are made specifically for Germany and Italy. The styling is top-of-the-line. Men's jackets come in every size and many styles. We especially like the bomber jackets, which sell for $200–$300. A comparable jacket in New York would be $750. Women's leather suits are a tad more expensive at $375–$500; but again, a suit of comparable quality would cost double in the United States. Stock up on leather pants in various colors ($150). The factory is to the right as you walk in, if you care to watch the work in progress. Hours are Monday–Saturday, 9:30 A.M. to 6 P.M.

SPLENDID, Sun Ping Industrial Building (7th floor), 916–922 Cheung Sha Wan Road, Kowloon

LEIGHTON STOCK SALES: Just down the street from Splendid you will see a big sign and an arrow pointing to the Stock Sales outlet. This is an especially fine resource for men. The whole back of the large showroom space is devoted to suits, pants, sweaters, and blazers. Styles are not way-out or European chic, but we saw some definite winners. Leighton Textiles Co. Ltd. is a huge contractor. A pair of nice wool pants was selling for $20. A great wool car coat was $50. There are even less expensive selections piled in the bins. Some pants were as low as $10. Leighton also sells women's and children's clothing, but we didn't get too excited about either. Hours are Monday–Saturday, 9 A.M. to 5 P.M.

LEIGHTON STOCK SALES, 868 Cheung Sha Wan Road, Kowloon

▼

AH CHOW PORCELAIN: Backtrack on Cheung Sha Wan Road until you see the alley between buildings 489 and 491. The entrance to Ah Chow is down this alley, which is really a driveway, in the building to your left. Be sure that you are in Block B before going to the 7th floor. Room numbers B1 and B2 will lead you to porcelain heaven. The showroom is crammed with huge jardinieres, waiting to go to a mansion or hotel, and lamps and vases of every size imaginable. Directly ahead from the entry is a room full of sample dishes. If you were a buyer for one of the major department stores, you would go in here and pick one from column A and one from column B. Many of the pieces on the floor have "Sold" signs (in Chinese, of course) on them. We asked; that's how we knew. If you look at the fine Chinese-style ashtrays, lamps, and ceramic goods in American department stores, you will recognize Ah Chow's merchandise. While they will make any pattern you want, or copy anything you want, it is easier to just pick from the overrun stock sitting around the shop. We shipped a set of ginger jars, and they arrived in perfect condition—wrapped better than a mummy. The shipping cost more than the jars, but who wants to hand-carry china for fifteen hours on a plane? If you buy a lamp, be sure to discuss the electrical current and type of plug you need. It may take a long time for your order to arrive, so be patient. We find this store to be quite honest in their business dealings.

The place is a little bit dusty, but this only adds to the charm. Breakables are piled high—don't bring the children! No credit cards are accepted, but traveler's checks are OK. Hours are Monday–Saturday, 10 A.M. to 7 P.M.

AH CHOW PORCELAIN, Hong Kong Industrial Centre, 489–491 Castle Peak Road, Block B (7th floor), Kowloon

▼

SANG WOO: Cross Cheung Sha Wan Road to get to Sang Woo. The building is located opposite the Leighton Textile Building, at number 883. Take the elevators to the 6th floor and turn right for Room 604. This is another great leather source with big- (and we mean BIG-) name designers represented . . . especially American. The outlet is air-conditioned (important in summer), and neatly arranged so you don't have to rummage. The biggest selections are in leather jackets for men. A bomber jacket sells for about $300. Soft leather pants were $200, and a chamois sweatshirt $100. This is upscale styling and prices. Try your luck and hope that a shipment has just arrived. There are also women's clothes. Hours are Monday–Friday, 9:30 A.M. to 5:30 P.M., Saturday to 12:30 P.M.

SANG WOO, Elite Building, 883 Cheung Sha Wan Road, Kowloon

LA TESSILE/LE BARON: This factory outlet is known by both names. To find the Yeung Yiu Chung Industrial Building, walk away from the main street, Cheung Sha Wan, on Cheung Lai Street. At the corner, one block away, turn right. No. 19 will be toward the beginning of the block. Enter through the garage and look on the wall for a sign that says "Yeung Yiu Chung (No. 6) Industrial Building." Take the elevators in the rear to the 7th floor to find the La Tessile factory. This is an honest factory. You will think for sure that we have sent you to the wrong place. However, point to the book and look lost. Someone in the office will come to rescue you. The factory shop is in the middle of the factory. You will be surrounded by knitting machines and boxes of finished cashmere sweaters. La Tessile manufactures the basic, warm variety of cashmere. No credit cards or traveler's checks. Bring cash. Hours are Monday–Friday, 9 A.M. to 5:30 P.M.; Saturday till noon.

LA TESSILE/LE BARON, Yeung Yiu Chung (No. 6) Industrial Building (7th floor), 19 Cheung Shun Street, Kowloon

▼

TEAM-LEE FASHION KNITTERS: Located in the same building but on the 9th floor, Team-Lee is a factory shop within the offices. You enter a very nice reception area, and the outlet is to the right, through glass doors. The knitwear here will make you wish you had a bigger suitcase. There are boxes and boxes of sweaters in colors and styles that are chic. You can find wool and cotton designs that are geometric or appliquéd. The styles change according to the season. We are sure these are private-label goods for great stores. Prices are fair, with the most expensive design costing under $300. Obviously, locals think this is outrageously expensive. No credit cards are accepted; cash only. Hours are Monday–Saturday, 9 A.M. to 5:30 P.M. Everything closes for lunch from 12:30 P.M. to 2 P.M.

TEAM-LEE FASHION KNITTERS, Yeung Yiu Chung (No. 6) Industrial Building (9th floor), 19 Cheung Shun Street, Kowloon

▼

BROADWAY SPORTSWEAR: Broadway Sportswear is located on the other side of Cheung Sha Wan Road. To get there, cross over to the MTR station and take a left to Tung Chau West Street. Take a right here and walk two blocks to Wing Hong Street, where you take another left to reach No. 7. Easier still, simply take a taxi. The building has a huge sign on top that says "Broadway," so once you are close you can't miss it. You will be more than pleased that you came. Broadway Sportswear is the single best source for designer raincoats in Hong Kong and Kowloon. The labels read like a *Who's Who* of European and American design.

The inside of Broadway is massive and confusing. Don't make this your last stop when you are already tired, or you will turn around and walk out. To the left of the entrance are racks of coats and jackets. Some of them are regular sports coats (for a major U.S. label); some are sports jackets and skiwear. A men's khaki sports coat in cotton was selling for $20 and a wool tweed blazer was $50. The tweedy country look is very prominent since the fashions are those of one particular designer label. Along the side and back walls are the raincoats, heavier coats, and still more jackets. A major-designer–label raincoat, which we saw in Bloomingdale's the season before, was one third the price here. It was a sample size. A wool-and-fur designer overcoat was $500. We happen to know this designer's coats never sell for under $1,000. There are coats with major department store labels and coats with major designer labels. We love this outlet. Hours are Monday–Saturday, 9:30 A.M. to 5:30 P.M. Closed for lunch from 1 P.M. to 2 P.M.

BROADWAY SPORTSWEAR, 7 Wing Hong Street (ground floor), Kowloon

Index of Stores by Neighborhood

Hong Kong

Central, Hong Kong

CONNAUGHT ROAD CENTRAL

MANDARIN ORIENTAL HOTEL

Fashion
Giorgio Armani, p. 171; Eddie Lau, p. 189

Leathergoods
Fendi, p. 177; Ferragamo, p. 177; Mayer Shoe Company, p. 215

Jewelry
Gemsland, p. 202, 220; Kai Yin Lo, pp. 189–190; K. S. Sze & Sons, p. 224

Tailors
A-Man Hing Cheong Company Ltd, p. 200; David's Shirts, pp. 202–203

P. C. LU & SONS, LTD., *Antiques/Home Furnishings,* p. 251

SWIRE HOUSE

Fashion
Bottega Veneta, p. 172; Kenzo, p. 185; Tokio Kumagai, p. 185; Matsuda, pp. 185–186; Moschino, p. 180; Issey Miyake, p. 186; Ragence Lam, pp. 188–189; Camberley, p. 92–93

Tailors
H. Baroman Ltd., pp. 199–200

Antiques/Home Furnishings
Grenley's, p. 239

CHATER ROAD

PRINCE'S BUILDING

Fashion
Chanel, p. 174; Christian Dior Monsieur,

DES VOEUX ROAD CENTRAL

ALEXANDRA HOUSE

THE LANDMARK

Causeway Bay, Hong Kong

LOCKHART ROAD

SOGO, *Department Store,* p. 166
MITSUKOSHI, *Department Store,* pp. 164–165

YEE WO STREET

PALIBURG PLAZA
Fashion: Hong Kong Designer's Gallery, pp. 192–193; Ben Yeung, p. 190

PATERSON STREET

MATSUZAKAYA, *Department Store,* p. 164
DAIMARU, *Department Store,* p. 163

HING FAT STREET

ESPRIT, *Fashion,* p. 182

Quarry Bay, Hong Kong

KING'S ROAD

CITYPLAZA II and III
Department Stores
　　Marks & Spencer, p. 158; Uny, p. 158; Wing On, p. 158
Fashion
　　Esprit, p. 182
Arts & Crafts
　　Amazing Grace, p. 158

TAIKOO SHING ROAD

JUSCO, *Department Store,* p. 158

Kowloon

Tsim Sha Tsui, Kowloon

CANTON ROAD

ESCADA, *Fashion,* p. 176

HARBOUR CITY/OCEAN TERMINAL

Fashion
Diane Freis, pp. 182–183; Alain Manoukian, p. 154; Lancel, pp. 216–217

Antiques/Home Furnishings
Hunter's, p. 239; Charlotte Horstmann & Gerald Godfrey, Ltd., p. 251

Arts & Crafts
Mountain Folkcraft, pp. 245–246

Jewelry
Axessorium, p. 222

Other
Toys "Я" Us, p. 185

HARBOUR CITY/OCEAN CENTRE

Fashion
Emporio Armani, p. 171; Cacharel, p. 173; Courrèges, p. 174; Jean-Paul Gaultier, p. 177; Trussardi, p. 181; M Group, pp. 194–195; Dorfit, pp. 164–165

Arts & Crafts
Amazing Grace Elephant Co., pp. 244–245

Department Store
Marks & Spencer, p. 168

HARBOUR CITY/OCEAN GALLERIES

Fashion
Diane Freis, pp. 182–183

Arts & Crafts
Banyan Tree, p. 246

Department Store
Marks & Spencer, p. 168

Lai Chi Kok, Kowloon

CHEUNG SHUN STREET

CHEUNG SHA WAN ROAD

WING HONG STREET

CASTLE PEAK ROAD

TUNG CHAU WEST STREET

Hung Hom, Kowloon

MAN YUE STREET

5 ▼ MYSTERIES OF HONG KONG

An Alphabetical Guide

ANTIQUES: An antique is any item of art, furniture, or craft work that is over 100 years old. The problem is proving it. There is no governing body in Hong Kong that "officially" proclaims an item to be over 100 years of age. There are many agencies that look and sound official, and have official papers, stamps, and seals, but none of them are government sanctioned. In Hong Kong, anything goes. This is very frustrating for the consumer who is trying to determine a fair value for a piece of art.

True antiques are a hot commodity, and unscrupulous dealers take advantage of that need by issuing authenticity papers for goods that are not old. To make matters worse, Hong Kong does not require its dealers to put prices on their goods. Depending on the dealer's mood, or assessment of your pocketbook, the ginger jar you love could cost $150 or $100.

Only you can determine if you feel like you're getting a good deal. Pick a reputable dealer, and ask a lot of questions about the piece, its period, etc. If the dealer doesn't know, and doesn't offer to find out, he probably is not a true antiques expert. Get as much in writing as possible. Even if it means nothing, it is proof that you have been defrauded if later you find out your Ming vase was made in Kowloon, circa 1989. Your invoice should contain what you are buying, age of item (including dynasty, year), where it was made, and any flaws or repairs done to the piece.

CAMERAS: There is a camera glut in Hong Kong. Knowing where and what to buy requires a little work on your part. Start by doing research at home as to what equipment you need. Do NOT allow a Hong Kong camera salesman to tell you what he thinks you should buy, or what is a good deal. Once you feel comfortable that you know what you are looking for, visit at least three shops and compare prices. We have discovered that prices can vary by as little as $10 and as much as $200 before negotiations begin. Be sure that you ascertain that the price for the camera includes a worldwide guarantee. You can get the same camera without the guarantee, and the price will be considerably less. The first time you have the camera fixed and get the bill you'll realize why it was such a bargain.

As soon as you start serious negotiations, examine the camera very carefully. It should still be in its original box, complete with styrofoam that packs it tightly. Remember that camera boxes can be repacked. Check to make sure yours was not. Look at the guarantee to verify that it is a worldwide guarantee and is authentic. There must be a stamp from the importing agent on the registration card. The dealer will add his stamp upon conclusion of the sale. If you are really careful you will call the importing agent and verify the sale. Check the serial numbers on the camera and lens with those on the registration card to make sure that they match. Take out the guarantee before the camera is repacked and ask to have it repacked in front of you. No bait and switch will happen this way. Ask to have the following information included in the store receipt: name and model of camera; serial numbers of parts; price of each item; date of purchase; itemized cost of purchase with total sum at the bottom; and form of payment you are using.

CARPETS: As the Persian carpet market has dried up, the popularity of Chinese carpets, both new and old, has escalated. China still has a labor pool of young girls who will work for very little money and sit for long periods of time tying knots. Carpets come in traditional designs or can be special-ordered. Price depends on knots per square inch, fiber content, complexity of design, how many colors are used, and city or region of origin. Any of the Chinese Arts & Crafts Stores is a good place to look at carpets and get familiarized with different styles and price ranges. You can visit the Tai Ping Carpet showroom in Central and then make an appointment to visit the factory in Kowloon (see page 248) to watch work in progress.

When considering the material of the rug, consider its use. Silk rugs are magnificent and impractical. If you are going to use the carpet in a low-traffic area or as a wall hanging, great. Silk threads are usually woven as the warp (vertical) threads and either silk or cotton as the weft (horizontal). The pile, nonetheless, will be pure silk. Wool rugs are more durable.

Chinese rugs come in every imaginable combination of colors. No one combination is more valuable than the next. Some older carpets have been colored with pure vegetable dyes; more modern ones use sturdier synthetics in combination with vegetable dyes. Avoid carpets that were made with aniline dyes, since these are unstable. To test for aniline dye, spit on a white handkerchief and then rub the cloth gently over the colors. If only a little color comes off you are safe. If the carpet has been dyed with aniline dyes, you will get a lot of color. These dyes were used on older rugs that were crafted at the beginning of the century.

CERAMICS AND PORCELAIN: Ceramic and porcelain wares available in Hong Kong fall into three categories: British imports, new Chinese, and old Chinese. For current British china resources see pages 239–240. New Chinese pottery and porcelain is in high demand. Although much of the base material is being imported from Japan and finished in Hong Kong, it is still considered Chinese. Most factories will take orders directly. Otherwise you would do as well to shop Hollywood Road and the big Chinese Arts & Crafts emporiums and Wah Tung.

Porcelain is distinguished from pottery in that it uses china clay to form the paste. Modern designs are less elaborate than those used during the height of porcelain design in the Ming Dynasty (A.D. 1368–1644) but the old techniques are slowly being revived. Blue-and-white ware is still the most popular and can be found at the various Chinese government stores, including Chinese Arts & Crafts. Fakes abound; buy with care.

CHINESE NEW YEAR: The most important festival of the year, the Chinese New Year, falls on a different day in each of our years due to the lunar calendar. It is usually in the latter part of January. Each year is identified with an animal that gives character to those born under it. According to legend, when Buddha asked all of the animals to come to him, only twelve showed up. As a result he named the years after them. The animal signs are those of the Rat, Ox, Tiger, Rabbit, Dragon, Snake, Horse, Ram, Monkey, Cockerel, Dog, and Pig.

During the Chinese (Lunar) New Year, most stores will close. For a few days preceding the festivities, it is not unusual to find prices artificially raised in many local shops, as shopkeepers take advantage of the fact that the Chinese like to buy new clothing for the new year.

CHINESE SCROLLS: Part art and part communication, Chinese scrolls are decorative pieces of parchment paper, attached at both ends to round pieces of wood, against which they are rolled, containing calligraphy and art relating to history, a story, a poem, a lesson, or a message. Some scrolls are mostly art, with little calligraphy, but others are just the opposite. Being able to identify the author, or artist, makes the scroll more valuable, but it is usually not possible. Chinese scrolls make beautiful wall hangings, and are popular collector's pieces.

CLOISONNÉ: The art of cloisonné involves fitting decorative enamel between thin metal strips on a metal surface. The surface is then fired under just the right temperatures and the finish is glazed to a sheen. It sounds simple, but the handwork involved in laying the metal strips to form a complicated design, and then laying in the paint so that it does not run, is time-consuming and delicate, and takes training and patience to perform. Works by the very finest artists bring in large sums of money. But it is also possible to get a small vase for about $20. You can also find rings, bracelets, and earrings for good prices at most of the markets.

COMPUTERS: All the famous brands, makes, and models of computers can be found in Hong Kong, but you had better be computer literate to know if you are getting a better deal than you could get back home. Be sure to check the power capacity, voltage requirements, guarantees, and serial numbers of every piece you buy. Clones are also available, and at very good prices. However, "Buyer Beware" applies doubly in this category.

EMBROIDERY: The art of stitching decorations onto another fabric by hand or machine is known as embroidery. Stitches can be combined to make abstract or realistic shapes, sometimes of enormous complexity. Embroidered goods sold in Hong Kong include bed linens, chair cushions, tablecloths, napkins, runners, place mats, coasters, blouses, children's clothing, and robes. Traditionally embroidery has been handsewn. However, today there are machines that do most of the work. Embroidery threads are made from the finest silk to the heaviest yarn. One popular form of embroidered work sold in Hong Kong is whitework, or white-on-white embroidery. Most of it is done by machine, but the workmanship is very good. Hand-embroidered goods are hard to find today, and very expensive.

FURNITURE: Chinese antique furniture is based on purity of form, with decorative and interpretive patterns carved into the sides or backs. Many designs date back to the Shang period, to the early 17th century B.C.

Many of the older pieces of authentic Chinese furniture have been left to rot in warehouses, or are sitting in disrepair in the backs of shops. It takes an experienced eye to spot them.

Antique furniture is a hot collector's item. Dealers and collectors alike are scouring the shops and auction houses. It is better to find an unfinished piece and oversee its restoration, however, than to find one that has already been restored. If it has been, find out who did the work and what was done. Some unknowing dealers bleach the fine woods and ruin their value. Others put a polyurethanelike gloss on the pieces and make them unnaturally shiny.

If your taste doesn't run to the older pieces, the more modern furniture designs are also beautiful. The most popular pieces are made from rosewood, which is becoming harder to find, thus more expensive than other woods. If you are buying a rosewood piece it is smart to have it verified by an expert and not just take the word of the dealer.

If you do decide to buy, decide beforehand how you will get the piece home. If you are shipping it through the shop, verify the quality of their shipper and insurance. If you are shipping it yourself, call a shipper and get details before you begin to negotiate the price of the piece. You may be able to offset the cost of shipping by the amount of discount you receive.

HAPPY COATS: One of the hottest-selling tourist items is the happy coat, or jacket with a stand-up mandarin collar, usually made of embroidered silk with decorative flowers, animals, and birds. Happy coats can be extravagant and luxurious or simple and plain. They make great housecoats and are good souvenirs of Hong Kong. Many shops sell them already wrapped and ready to go.

IVORY: *We have a word of warning:* Articles made from ivory will not be allowed into the United States. It is not smart to try to run them.

Carvers in Hong Kong are currently using dentin from walrus, hippopotamuses, boars, and whales as ivory. If you want to make sure you are not buying elephant ivory, look for a network of fine lines that is visible to the naked eye. If the piece you are buying is made of bone, there will not be any visible grain or luster. Bone also weighs less than ivory. Imitation ivory is made of plastic, but can be colored to look quite good. However, it is a softer material than real ivory, and less dense. Many *netsuke* that you find in the markets are made of bone dust or plastic.

There are very few antique ivory pieces left in Hong Kong. If someone claims to be selling you one, be very wary. Should you snag one, you'll need provenance papers to bring it into the U.S.

JADE: The term *jade* is used to signify two different stones, jadeite and nephrite. The written character for jade signifies purity, nobility, and beauty. Jade has been revered in China for 5,000 years, and is available in many forms. It is considered by some to be a magical stone, protecting the health of one who wears it. The scholar always carried a piece of jade in his pocket for health and wisdom. Jade is also reported to pull the impurities out of the body.

Jadeite and nephrite have different chemical properties. Jadeite tends to be more translucent and nephrite more opaque. For this reason, jadeite is often considered to be more valuable.

Jadeite comes in many colors, including lavender, yellow, black, orange, red, pink, white, and many shades of green. Nephrite comes in varying shades of green only. The value of both is determined by translucence, quality of carving, and color. Assume that a carving that is too inexpensive is not jade. "Jade" factories work in soapstone or other less valuable stones. The Jade Market (see page 140) is a fun adventure and a good way to look at lots of "fake" and real jade. Test your eye before you buy. If you are determined to buy a piece of genuine jade, we suggest that you use a trusted jeweler or other reputable source (such as the Chinese Arts & Crafts Stores or the jade boutique in the Lane Crawford department store); you'll pay more than you might in a market or a small jewelry shop, but you'll be paying for peace of mind.

NETSUKE: A *netsuke* is a Japanese-style carving, usually small, of an ornamental figure. *Netsuke* were originally designed to enable the kimono wearer, who has no pockets, to carry a small case looped over the belt. The *netsuke* was fastened to the kimono belt with a short cord. The quality of the carving indicated the importance of the wearer. Most old *netsuke* are carved out of ivory, which is now illegal to import into the United States. New *netsuke* figures are being made in Hong Kong, carved out of bone or plastic. They are stained or colored to look old, but don't quite achieve the patina or grace of aged ivory. The current rage in Hong Kong is *netsuke* of erotic figures. The carvings are somewhat coarse and usually made from bone, stained or watercolored for that old look.

NINTENDO: When Castlevania III was hot news in the States, in Hong Kong you could already get Castlevania IV. You can find game cartridges with eighty-two games in one cartridge (about $100). Some of the familiar American games have different titles in their Hong Kong versions. For instance, Mega Man is called Rock Man in Hong Kong, and Power Mission is Power Blazer. With prices at a fraction of U.S. prices, who cares? Typical Hong Kong price for Mario III: $25. This game costs $50 in the U.S. You'll also find a bigger selection of games you haven't heard of than you might imagine. When in doubt, just go by what looks good. You can always try games in the store. If you are planning on buying any Nintendo games in Hong Kong, have an up-to-date *Nintendo Power* issue with you so you can show it to salespeople, who might be able to match up the games in case of different names.

You must buy a converter ($8–$10) in order to use Japanese-style game cartridges on a U.S. Nintendo, because you can't use the Japanese size on your machine. The converter attaches to the cartridge to make it compatible with your machine. This is technology at its best. Take advantage of the opportunity to get a new game, and get something your friends don't have. You can have games before anybody else gets them. Buy the converter in Hong Kong, because they aren't sold in Japan.

OPALS: Hong Kong is considered the opal-cutting capital of Asia. Dealers buy opals, which are mined mainly in Australia, in their rough state, and bring them to their factories in Hong Kong. There they are judged for quality and then cut either for wholesale export or for local jewelry. Black opals are the rarest, and therefore the most expensive. White opals are the most available; they are not actually white but varying shades of sparkling color. The opal has minuscule spheres of cristobalite layered inside; this causes the light to refract and the gem to look iridescent. The more cristobalite, the more "fire." An opal can contain up to 30% water, which makes it very difficult to cut. Dishonest dealers will sell sliced stones, called doublets or triplets depending upon the number of slices of stone layered together. If the salesman will not show you the back of the stone, suspect that it is layered. There are several opal "factories" in Hong Kong. These shops offer tourists the chance to watch the craftsmen at work cutting opal, and offer opal jewelry for sale at "factory" prices. It's an interesting and informative tour to take, but we couldn't vouch for the quality of any opal you might buy from a factory. Again, it's best to trust a reputable jeweler if you wish to buy a quality stone.

PAPERCUTS: An art form still practiced in China, papercuts are handpainted and handcut drawings of butterflies, animals, birds, flowers, and human figures. Often they are mounted on cards; sometimes they are sold in packs of six, delicately wrapped in tissue. We buy them in quantity and use them as decorations on our own cards and stationery.

PEARLS: The first thing to know about pearls is that the best ones come from Japan. If you are looking for a serious set of pearls, find a dealer who will show you the Japanese government inspection certification that is necessary for every legally exported pearl. Many pearls cross the border without this, and for a reason.

Pearls are usually sold loosely strung and are weighed by the *momme*. Each *momme* is equal to 3.75 grams. The size of the pearls is measured in millimeters. Size 3s are small, like caviar, and 10s are large, like mothballs. The average buyer is looking for something between 6 and 7 millimeters. The price usually doubles every ½mm after 6. Therefore, if a

6mm pearl is $10, a 6½mm pearl would be $20, a 7mm $40, and so on. When the size of the pearl gets very high, prices often triple and quadruple with each ½mm.

Most pearls you will encounter are cultured. The pearl grower introduces a small piece of mussel shell into the oyster, and then hopes that Mother Nature will do her stuff. The annoyed oyster coats the "intruder" with nacre, the lustrous substance that creates the pearl. The layers of nacre determine the luster and size. It takes about five years for an oyster to create a pearl. The oysters are protected from predators in wire baskets in carefully controlled oyster beds.

There are five basic varieties of pearls: freshwater, South Seas, *akoya*, black, and *mabe.* **FRESHWATER PEARLS** are also known as Biwa pearls, and are the little Rice Krispies–shaped pearls that come in shades of pink, lavender, cream, tangerine, blue, and blue-green. Many of the pearls larger than 10mm are known as **SOUTH SEAS PEARLS.** They are produced in the South Seas, where the water is warmer and the oysters larger. The silver-lipped oyster produces large, magnificent silver pearls. The large golden-colored pearls are produced by the golden-lipped oyster. The pearls you are probably most familiar with are known as **AKOYA PEARLS.** These range from 2mm to 10mm in size. The shapes are more round than not, and the colors range from shades of cream to pink. A few of these pearls have a bluish tone. The rarest pearl is the **BLACK PEARL,** which is actually a deep blue or blue-green. This gem is produced by the black-lipped oyster of the waters surrounding Tahiti and Okinawa. Sizes range from 8mm to 15mm. Putting together a perfectly matched set is difficult and costly. **MABE PEARLS** (pronounced maw-bay) have flat backs and are considered "blister" pearls because of the way they are attached to the shell. They are distinguished by their silvery bluish tone and rainbow luster.

Pearls are judged by their luster, nacre, color, shape, and surface quality. The more perfect the pearl in all respects, the more valuable.

SEGA: Ditto section on Nintendo. If you are buying for a child and are not personally familiar with all aspects of the game cartridges, bring a U.S. game with you so you can make sure you buy a compatible game tape.

SILK: The art of weaving silk originated some 4,000 years ago in China. Since that time it has spread throughout Asia and the world. China, however, remains the largest exporter of cloth and garments. Hong Kong receives most of its silk fabric directly from China. Fabric shops in the markets sell rolls of silk for reasonable prices. Try Wing On Street (Cloth Alley) or Li Yuen East and West. Embroidered silk fabric is also very popular, and can be found in the Chinese Arts & Crafts Stores around the city. Silk is graded according to evenness of weave, strength, color clarity, and elasticity. Be sure, when buying silk, that it is real. Many wonderful copies are on the market today. Real silk thread burns like human hair and leaves a fine ash. Synthetic silk curls or melts as it burns. If you are not sure, remove a thread and light a match.

SNUFF BOTTLES: A favorite collector's item, snuff bottles come in porcelain, glass, stone, metal, bamboo, bronze, and jade. The glass bottles with a carved overlay are rare and magnificent. There are schools of snuff bottles that are especially valuable to collect. You can find more ordinary examples in any of the markets.

SPORTS SHOES: If you haven't shopped with a preteen, you might not know just how important it is to be wearing the "right" sports shoes to school. Much of our time in Hong Kong was spent discussing the Pump (a type of shoe made by Reebok) and the various copycat styles. Since the Pump costs over $100 in the U.S., there is some hope for a deal in Hong Kong. Indeed, there are tons of name-brand sports shoes sold everywhere—from stores to Stanley Market to street. For the most part, they cost 20% more than they do in the U.S. We know they are made in Korea and should be cheap, but so far our findings have been sorry.

If you must buy the Pump, do so in the U.S. where you know what you are getting. If your child will be satisfied with a high-style substitute, you'll have many choices. Expect to pay over $50, though. You can still do better at Marshall's at home!

TEA: The Museum of Tea Ware in Flagstaff House, Cotton Tree Drive, Central, Hong Kong, is a good place to start an exploration into the mysteries of tea. Teahouses are popular in Hong Kong. Don't be surprised to see many people at the tables accompanied by their birds.

Varieties of Chinese tea are almost unlimited. Tea has been grown in China for over 2,000 years, and reflects the climate and soil where it is grown, much as European wines do. There are three categories of tea: green or unfermented tea, red or fermented tea, and semi-fermented tea. It is customary to drink Chinese tea black, with no milk, sugar, or lemon. Cups do not have a handle but often do have a fitted lid to keep the contents hot and to strain the leaves as you sip. Since Hong Kong is a British colony, you may also find many hotel lobbies and restaurants that serve an English high tea (a great opportunity to rest your feet and gear up for a few more hours of shopping).

YIXING POTTERY TEAPOTS: Tea utensils are a popular item to purchase in Hong Kong, with Yixing pottery teapots being one of the most popular and expensive. They are made from unglazed purple clay and are potted by hand to achieve different forms of balance. They often resemble leaves, trees, or animals.

Proportion is achieved by changing the balance of the base, top, and handle. Yixing teapots are always signed by the artist who made them, and the more famous artists' pots sell for over $1,000.

6▼ TO MARKET, TO MARKET

Market Heaven

Hong Kong is market heaven. There are fruit and vegetable markets, general merchandise markets, jade markets, thieves', ladies', and men's markets. There are market lanes and market areas. There is even a market city.

Markets are a way of life in Hong Kong, and we love them. But they are a very real slice of life. They are not pretty or fancy. If you have a squeamish stomach, avoid the food markets that sell live chickens or ducks and slaughter them on the spot. Many visitors who have only seen chicken wrapped in cellophane find this distasteful. But it is the way of life in Hong Kong. Open-air food markets like Jardine's Bazaar are a little easier to take than indoor ones, like Central Market, where the sights and smells are intense. Merchandise markets are busy and hectic. There are no spacious aisles or racks of organized clothing. Some markets exist only for certain hours of the day or night. At a pre-appointed time, people appear from nowhere, pushing carts laden with merchandise. They set up shop along the street, selling their goods until the crowds start to dissipate, at which time they disappear into the night. It is fun to get to a market like Ladies' Market before the unofficial opening time to watch it set up.

Markets have their own rules, just like stores. If you want to be successful at bargaining and come home with good buys, we offer a few suggestions:

▼ Dress simply. The richer you look, the higher the starting price. Most goods on carts do not have price tags. If you have an engagement ring that broadcasts RICH AMERICAN, turn it around, or leave it in the hotel safe. We like to wear blue jeans and T-shirts to the market. We still look like visitors, but no one can tell what our budget is.

▼ Check with your hotel concierge about the neighborhood where the market is located. It may not be considered safe for a woman to go there alone, or after dark. We don't want to sound chauvinistic or paranoid, but crime in market areas can be higher than in tourist areas—especially at the night markets.

▼ Carry the local currency and have a lot of change with you. Most market shops or stalls do not take credit cards. It's also difficult to bargain and then offer a large bill and ask for change. As a bargaining point, be able to say you only have so much cash on hand.

▼ Branded merchandise sold on the street can be hot, counterfeit, or of inferior quality.

▼ Sizes may not be true to the tags.

▼ Go early if you want the best selection. Go late if you want to make the best deals.

▼ Never trust anyone who does business from the street to mail anything for you.

▼ Don't give your hotel address to anyone who wants to bring you some other samples the next day.

▼ Make sure you are buying something you can legally bring back to the States. Don't buy ivory; all varieties are illegal to import. Don't buy tortoiseshell; it will be impounded by Customs.

▼ Don't think less of yourself if you end up paying the asking price. Things are changing in Hong Kong, and some vendors will not budge.

Most markets have no specific street address, but are known by a set of streets that intersect the beginning or the middle of the market area. The majority of cab drivers know where the markets are by name. However, it is always a good precaution to have your concierge write the name of the market and location in Chinese before you leave. You probably won't need it, but it can't hurt. Buses, trolleys, and the MTR usually service the markets as well. Your concierge can give you exact directions from your hotel. Take a hotel business card with you, so you'll have the address in Chinese in case you need directions back home.

STANLEY MARKET
Stanley Main Street, Stanley Village, Hong Kong

Stanley Market is world-renowned. Any tourist coming to Hong Kong knows about Stanley. Shopping legends abound about fabulous bargains on designer clothing. After all the buildup, we find the reality a bit disappointing. Since honesty is the name of our game, we are going to tell you the truth about Stanley Market: Stanley ain't what it used to be.

Don't get us wrong. We love Stanley Market. It is located in a beautiful part of Hong Kong Island. There are more tourist goods here than anywhere else. You have concentrated shopping for just about anything you might want to buy. It's fun, it's clean, and it's festive; but you will pay for the privilege. You will probably overpay for the privilege.

We have received a number of angry letters from people who were annoyed that they spent the time and money to go to Stanley, felt that it was expensive and a waste of time. On the other hand, we still love Stanley.

First of all, if you are traveling with children, Stanley is great entertainment for them. It's safe, it seems exotic (to them), they can wander a little but not get lost, and there is merchandise for sale that interests them—including souvenirs, toys, and running shoes.

Now then, plain and simple: Stanley is a tourist trap. Prices may be higher than elsewhere; vendors are less likely to bargain with you. We've been set up in Stanley, we've been cheated, we've been disappointed in love (of an item, not a person). That's why Stanley is so much fun.

We do know locals who shop here, and our friend Rose swears that if you come often and shop carefully, you can find some good buys.

One of the reasons we like Stanley so much is that we love the ride. If you have the time, go on the bus and return by taxi (since you will have a lot of packages). You can go with your car and driver and make a stop at Repulse Bay to see the elegant shopping there in the minimall (109 Repulse Bay Road); you may also want to go for a swim in the lovely little bay right before you get to Stanley. There is a public beach. If all you care about is the shopping, don't arrive before 9:30 or 10 A.M., as the vendors don't really set up too early.

We usually travel to Stanley by the No. 6 or No. 260 bus, which leaves from the Central Bus Terminus or in front of the Star Ferry terminal, and takes about forty-five minutes in moderate traffic.

You can start your tour of Stanley Market at Watson's and use it as a landmark in case you get separated from friends or family. (They also have rest rooms.) From Watson's, walk straight down Stanley New Street toward the water, and when you reach the main street of the market choose left or right. We usually go left first, and explore the main market street, then the alleys that lead up the hill. The restaurants are located in this area. If you are really in a hurry there are fast-food stands in the market as well. When you retrace your steps along the main street and continue on the other side of Stanley New Street, you will have a beautiful view of the beach and can stop to take pictures. You can take a right on Stanley Market Road and circle around back to Watson's and the taxi stand afterwards. The main street is where you can expect to find your more substantial purchases. These shops are housed in buildings, and have been in the same location for years. Many of them take credit cards and traveler's checks. If not, there are two banks on Main Street.

If you haven't bought too much to carry and are taking the bus home, the stop is across the main road at the top of the market. Ask for directions. You can get off at Admiralty to connect to the MTR. Market hours are seven days a week, 10 A.M. to 7 P.M.

LADIES' MARKET (MONG KOK MARKET)
Argyle Street and Nathan Road, Mong Kok, Kowloon

The market sets up a short distance away from the Mong Kok MTR station. The streets have the feeling of a carnival, with lots of people parading by the stands, stopping to examine shirts, socks, sewing sets, buttons, and bras. There are some toys and sunglasses, but mostly lots of trinkets, shirts, socks, and everyday goods. This market is not a great one; there are no live snakes, however.

Getting there is easy on the MTR. Take the train from Central, Admiralty, or Tsim Sha Tsui to Mong Kok. Exit in the direction of Sincere Department Store. Cross Sai Yeung Choi and turn right on Tung Choi. This is where the market begins. Walk on Tung Choi until it dead-ends into Dundas. If you turn right and cross Sai Yeung Choi again you will be on Nathan Road. Mong Kok station will be to your right, and Yau Ma Tei to your left. There will be more action on the other side of the station as well, toward Mong Kok Street.

TEMPLE STREET MARKET
(KOWLOON NIGHT MARKET/
THIEVES' MARKET)
Temple Street and Jordan Road, Kowloon

This market has as many names as personalities. It has been growing over the years, due as much to the popularity of the street scene that happens around it as to the merchandise. On any given night you will find an endless variety of everyday shirts, socks, jewelry, homeware, and children's clothing. We got a great deal on a suitcase for $25. The market is extremely crowded, with people pushing and shoving to get past. If you are nervous in crowds, don't go. Don't carry a lot of cash. Dress down; don't carry a purse. And just enjoy the action.

We especially like the cultural scene that happens on some of the back streets. You can peek into the mah-jong parlors and listen to the clacking of the tiles and the hollering of the players; you can get your fortune told; you can watch as the amateur opera singers perform famous Chinese operas; you can watch magicians do their tricks, be treated by an acupuncturist or acupressurist, or watch a dentist plying his trade at curbside.

Getting to this market is very simple. Take the MTR to the Jordan Road station. Exit toward Yue Hwa Department Store. At the exit turn right and walk three blocks to Temple Street. Take a right again on Temple Street; you will see the market begin. Follow the market as it goes in a U back to where you started. Hours are from 8 P.M. to midnight.

JADE MARKET
Kansu and Battery streets, Yau Ma Tei, Kowloon

The Jade Market is a day market where you will find your best buys on those little green (or violet or pink) stones that everyone will expect you to bring home. The scene varies according to the day, time, and season. One time we went, it was so crowded we could hardly squeeze our way in to look; another time, we were the only ones there. We can't guarantee what you will find, but we do know that you won't be disappointed if you are looking for variety and a chance to hone your bargaining skills.

The market is located in an enclosed area that used to be a playground at Kansu and Battery streets. An outside market takes place around the enclosed one at Reclamation Street. Here you will find "unofficial" stone dealers, clothing salesmen, and just about everything else. Across Reclamation Street is the large Yau Ma Tei Food Market.

The Jade Market is an official market organized by the Hong Kong and Kowloon Jade Merchants Workers' and Hawkers' Union Association. Each merchant inside the fence is licensed to sell jade, and should display his license above his stall. It is a good idea when buying to note the number next to your purchase, just in case you have a problem later on and the jade turns out to be plastic.

If you are hoping to buy quality jade, there are a few things to check. Make sure that the color is pure and strong. There should be no hint of black (unless the jade is black) or yellow. If the color is translucent, that is a good sign of value. Make sure that the color is as even as possible. A carving will have variations, but a jade circle should not. Also, check for fault lines. A good piece of jade will not have them. If any of the above faults appear in the piece of jade you are buying, bargain accordingly. (See page 127 for more information on jade.)

As you walk into the market, stop and get your bearings. The area is laid out in rows of carts, back to back in the middle and around the perimeter. We like to do one walk through before we get serious. There is more for sale than just jade, so keep your eyes open for other good buys. One year we bought lapis beads, and another time inexpensive colored-stone necklaces. The jade merchants have very similar merchandise; it's just a matter of how much you want to spend and which one will make you the best deal. We go from cart to cart asking the price on the same item. As soon as the merchants get the gist of what we are doing the price starts coming down. This only works if the market is not crowded. On a crowded day, we usually follow a Chinese person around and watch how he or she conducts business. Most often, the asking price is written on a piece of paper; then the buyer's bargaining price is written after it; and so on. If your eyesight is good enough you can get an idea of what the item is worth, and then bargain the same way. The dealers have a special way of negotiating that is quite interesting. The one making the offer will shake hands under a newspaper with the one selling. At the same time, he will indicate with his fingers what he is offering. The seller will then reply in kind, using his fingers. No one can see what the negotiations represent. As soon as they remove their hands from under the paper the negotiations have been concluded. Bargaining is part of the system even among the traders.

If you are not willing to bargain here, don't buy. You will get the same, if not a better, price in the Chinese Arts & Crafts Stores, paying retail. The merchants in the Jade Market expect to lower their price by 20% to 40% depending on your bargaining skill and their need. We have always had our best luck by pulling out a single bill and saying, "This is all we have left." If the shopkeeper says no, we walk away and try again elsewhere. This method has never failed us yet. If you want to make the best deal, and are planning to buy a lot, stick with one vendor.

If you are a serious collector, there is another "unofficial market" that takes place around the corner on Canton Road. Canton Road crosses Kansu Street one block after Battery, toward the harbor. Walk away from Kansu Street until you see the retail jade sellers' shops. In front of them you will see groups of men quietly dealing stones. Stand back and watch the method, which is very secretive. If you didn't know, you would think that they were simply having a conversation. You need to know your jade to deal here.

To get to the "official" jade market, take the MTR to Jordan Road and walk toward Yue Hwa Department Store. Take a left and then another left to get onto Nathan Road. Walk five blocks toward the underpass and then take another left onto Kansu Street. You will see the market ahead of you, two blocks farther down.

Market hours are 10 A.M. to 4 P.M., although many of the vendors close up shop at 2 P.M. Go early rather than late.

JARDINE'S BAZAAR
Causeway Bay, Hong Kong

If you stay in Causeway Bay, you have a foot up on the rest of the world when it comes to Jardine's Bazaar, Jardine's Lookout (a hillside residential area), and the web of streets between the two. This is what we came to China for. The first half of the market is full of fruit, vegetables, and other foodstuffs. At midpoint Jardine's becomes a dry-goods market and sells the same stuff you'll find everywhere. Jardine's is also in a home-sewing neighborhood, so you may enjoy wandering around looking at fabrics and notions, which are upstairs.

CENTRAL MARKET
Queen's Road Central, Hong Kong

The major food and produce markets for Hong Kong Island are located in specific areas. Central Market serves the area of Central. As you get even remotely close to Central Market on a sunny summer day, you will know where you are. The air will smell pungent and ripe. Central Market is located in a three-story warehouse, and the ventilation is not terrific. As a result the odors waft onto the surrounding sidewalks. The market sells every variety of fresh produce and meat that you might imagine. There are three levels of gleaming vegetables and fruit, clucking chickens, and quacking ducks in cages waiting to be picked for dinner. We can only take a few minutes in here before we want to rescue all the caged animals. We do think that the market is fascinating, however, if you want a glimpse of the real Hong Kong lifestyle.

KOWLOON CITY MARKET
Lion Rock Road, Kowloon

This one is a bit far out, but is especially entertaining because this is where the young locals like to hang out. Merchandise is a little more with-it; there's more fun in the air. This is one of the few markets where you'll find china sold. There are lots of blue jeans, factory-outlet rejects, and fashions from young Japanese and Chinese designers. This market only operates during the day. We like going after lunch to make sure that it is hopping.

CAT STREET MARKET
Central, Hong Kong

Cat Street Market is also known as the Thieves' Market or Ladder Street Market. Originally, many of the goods set out on the blankets were hot off a truck, and the sellers could gather them up quickly if the authorities came around. Now the market is more pedestrian, with many of the goods being from homes, but legally so. You will find hubcaps, refrigerator doors, old radios, and toilets, along with antiques and jade. The shops behind and around the market specialize in formal antiques and have some wonderful pieces. After you pass the Man Mo Temple on Hollywood Road, turn right onto Ladder Street. Down Ladder Street and on Upper Lascar Road, you will see blankets covered with goods. There is an official Cat Street Market Building behind the street vendors, where you can buy furniture and antiques. The market operates during normal business hours. A must.

The Lanes

"The Lanes" is a collective term for a group of small markets set in streets and alleys—usually only one block long. Except for Pottinger Street, which is a stairway filled with booths, the Lanes are built between large buildings. They're sort of the Asian version of the Burlington Arcade in London.

The Lanes are all in Central, and are within walking distance of each other. They are also near many other places in Central, so it's likely you will pass them in your daily travels.

LI YUEN STREET EAST: If you're looking for an inexpensive look-alike designer handbag, Li Yuen Street East is just the place. There are not a lot of inexpensive, high-quality leathergoods available in Hong Kong, and while Li Yuen Street East is not Neiman Marcus, it is the location of choice for locals who need handbags or briefcases. Expect to pay $40–$50 for a nice leather handbag of the current style or the Hermès flavor. If you look hard, you can even find a nice Chanel copy. It won't have the CC's, but the styling and design will be exact. Li Yuen Street East is also famous for its knitting shops, fabric stores, notions, and padded brassieres.

LI YUEN STREET WEST: Perhaps you want one of those satin quilted happy coats or vests that you associate with a trip to China. Li Yuen Street West is crammed with them.

Be sure to try them on, as the shoulders sometimes run small. Whatever you didn't see on Li Yuen Street East will be on Li Yuen Street West. To get to these two streets, follow the signs as you exit the Central MTR stop.

POTTINGER STREET: After a big lunch, give your leg muscles a workout and make the steep climb up Pottinger Street. There's nothing unusual for sale here—merely notions. However, we buy shoulder pads by the dozen. They are about half the cost. Notions are about 20% cheaper here than in a regular Hong Kong department store. If you buy jade circles for gifts, you can buy polyester or silk cord in rainbow colors in Pottinger Street. Hang the cord through the circle and you have a beautiful necklace. One meter of cord per necklace will be perfect.

MAN WA LANE: If you are looking for fun, Chinese atmosphere, and maybe some business cards in Chinese, don't miss Man Wa Lane. Man Wa Lane is headquarters of the chop business. But whether you are looking for chops or not, you should see this small, neat street, which spans about three blocks and has a few other stalls that sell general merchandise. If you do buy something from one of the shops and have to return for it, make sure you get a piece of paper with the shop address in both English and Chinese. The stalls do not have numbers but symbols, and they're all in Chinese. We tell you from embarrassed experience: You will never find your way back to a given stall unless you have the address in Chinese.

WING ON STREET: Known as Cloth Alley, this street is three blocks west of the Central Market, and is the place to go for the best buys on fabrics. Almost any type of fabric you might want is sold, from lightweight silks to heavy brocades. The market is open during the day; it feels like the two Li Yuen streets, but sells only fabrics.

7 ▾ HONG KONG HOTLINE

Shopping Centers/Shopping Buildings

Rumor has it that the shopping mall was invented in Hong Kong by a brilliant British tycoon who knew that all tourists want to go shopping and that rain prevents them from doing some of that shopping. Indeed, once you set shoe in any of the plethora of shopping centers and buildings you will not know—or care—if it is day or night, light or dark, winter or summer, rainy or dry outside.

Hong Kong is totally overrun with shopping centers. It's like a contagious disease spreading to all architects, who now feel compelled to equip a hotel or an office building with three floors of retail shops before they get to the actual offices. Somewhere, somehow, they find tenants for all those shops. While stores do come and go in these locations, and there is always some new rumor as to which location is hotter than any other, these shopping centers and buildings do offer all of the riches of the Orient under one roof.

The Cha-Cha Theory of Retailing

In our years of shopping Hong Kong, we have come to the conclusion that every retailer in town is constantly doing the cha-cha. Word spreads that a certain development, an area, a new mall, a building site will become hot (for whatever reasons) and suddenly, one, two, cha-cha-cha: everyone moves, or opens a branch store.

In their wake, a dozen dead dance partners lie panting on the streets. The Landmark, the greatest Hong Kong upscale mall of them all, is still holding its own. But other locations grow pale or become shadows of their former selves, taken over by local mom-and-pop shops while the glitzy showbirds amble off.

The hot "new" property in malls/buildings right now is Pacific Place, the shopping part of which is also known as The Mall at Pacific Place. We believe The Mall at Pacific Place will hold its own, not only because it has two huge and gorgeous hotels to anchor it, but because the Japanese department store Seibu has put in their first Hong Kong store. Seibu, in case you aren't up on Japanese department stores (see page 165) rhymes with "I love you."

If you go to a lot of the malls and shopping buildings, you'll see a huge amount of overlap. The stores all look alike (they are alike; you are not crazy), and soon the buildings themselves start to look alike (they really don't look alike). Your head swims. Your feet ache. Your brain shouts: "Why?"

We cannot tell you who will be leading the cha-cha next month, or that you will care. At a certain point, you choose your shopping by what buildings are convenient to you. We list the following directory of the main malls and shopping buildings in the order that we think is most current, interesting, and essential (all at the same time), so you can pick and choose according to your time frame and your location. We don't suggest that you try to do more than three malls unless you have a *lot* of patience and a lot of curiosity.

A corollary to the continuing cha-cha theory: Stores sometimes move around within a mall. Or malls can renumber the shops during a renovation—as they did in Harbour City. If you are seeking a specific store, ask at the information desk or use the directories. We were so lost in The Mall at Pacific Place, a relatively small space compared to something like Harbour City, that we almost cried. If you like to just wander, go: Enjoy. If you want to find something, ask.

Hotel Arcades

E ver since the 1950s, Holiday Inns of America has hosted little shops in their motel offices where you can buy toothpaste, aspirin, and tampons. Hotels in Hong Kong have taken this basic idea and carried it one step further. They have little shops in their lobbies—or in their arcade areas—that sell everything you might want or need. For life.

There are several reasons for the popularity of hotel arcades in Hong Kong. They're dry in rain; they're cool in summer (like shopping malls); they're handy for the tourist who will spend according to convenience; and, most important, they receive the benefits of trust. Shoppers have come to judge the shops in a hotel to be as reliable as the hotel itself. Thus the fanciest, most deluxe hotels have the most trustworthy shops. Shoppers believe there is a direct correlation between the quality of the store and the quality of the hotel.

Certainly the shops in the Peninsula, the Mandarin Oriental, and the Regent are the most expensive and most exclusive. But that doesn't mean there's anything wrong with the shops in the Holiday Inn. Some hotel arcades offer a handful of shops. Others have three levels of stores and hundreds of choices. Often, a hotel arcade connects to a main shopping center. From the Omni Prince Hotel at the far end of Harbour City, you can walk through a shopping arcade to connect to the Omni Marco Polo Hotel, and then go into another shopping center and keep on connecting for a few miles, several hotels, and thousands of stores, and end up at Omni The Hong Kong Hotel.

The Rise of the Regent

I n the old days, The Peninsula Hotel was the *grande dame* of Kowloon, and its shopping arcade was the famous residence of the biggest and best local and international names. The climate at the Peninsula has changed, and while the stores remain well-bred, the clients the Peninsula (and its stores) once depended on have moved across the street to the Regent.

The Regent has absolutely no shopping in the lobby itself, but adjoins not one but two shopping malls: The Regent Shopping Arcade and New World Shopping Centre, a multilevel mall with a Japanese department store anchor (**TOKYU**). The two levels of shopping space at the Regent are so new, fresh, and spacious compared to the Peninsula that the elegant crowd has switched over—now there are branch stores of every international big name you can think of at the Regent.

Does the world of Hong Kong need two Chanel boutiques, a block apart? Apparently so. But shoppers who do not will find the Regent's selection of forty or fifty stores to be the cream of the crop and an easy way to see upscale Hong Kong in one fell swoop. If you're looking to test one hotel arcade, look to the Regent. If you want a mall, try Pacific Place.

Directory of Malls, Buildings, and Hotel Arcades

THE MALL AT PACIFIC PLACE: This is the hottest location in town, the one that made everyone do the cha-cha.

Enter The Mall at Pacific Place, as it is officially known, through the Admiralty MTR, but avoid the Admiralty Shopping Centre (see page 160) or you will become depressed. The nicest approach is from either the Marriott Hotel or the Conrad Hotel, or from your limousine, but of course the MTR will do just fine. You may also take a tram to the Queensway stop.

The mall is small, as Hong Kong malls go, but confusing because it has different orbits. You might not mind getting lost, but don't miss the various parts of the complex out of ignorance or confusion.

This upscale mall offers a hefty dose of everything you want to see, including a small but good **LANE CRAWFORD** and the first **SEIBU** Japanese department store in Hong Kong. Most stores are open 10 A.M. to 8 P.M. daily, although not every store is open on Sunday, and the stores that do open on Sunday usually open at 1 P.M. There are a few gourmet food stores (**OLIVER'S**), some antiques shops (**C. P. CHING**), some eateries, including an American barbeque restaurant (**DAN RYAN**), and the usual big names like **ALFRED DUNHILL, BOSS, ERMENEGILDO ZEGNA, DAVIDOFF, BALLANTYNE, CARLOS FALCHI, KAI YIN LO, JOSEPH HO STUDIO, ZOE COSTE, DANIEL HECHTER, DIANE FREIS,** and **MARGUERITE LEE.** There are also more casual chains, such as **THE ATHLETE'S FOOT, THE BODY SHOP, CITY CHAIN** (watches), **BENETTON,** and **CROCO-KIDS.**

THE MALL AT PACIFIC PLACE, 88 Queensway, Hong Kong (MTR: Admiralty)

THE LANDMARK: The most famous of the Central centers, The Landmark has the reputation and the big names but is having to fight to stay ahead of the game. Many of the big names that started here have remained, but have opened other shops around town, so they are are no longer exclusively in The Landmark. Surely the mall is a must for visitors, who will be awestruck by the glitz and the fountain and the money it takes to make a place like this work.

The multilevel mall is topped by Gloucester and Edinburgh towers. We often suggest this mall as a jumping-off place for Westerners who want to see something but aren't quite ready for Kowloon. After a quick survey you'll probably find that everything is gorgeous but very expensive, and that you are ready to move on. There are a few cafés here for lunch. There is a Pizza Hut as well as a supermarket in the basement, the air-conditioning is nice, the central location in Central is a winner, and you're just across the street from discount shopping in the Pedder Building (page 159) if that's more to your taste.

Among the upscale and big-name tenants you'll find **HERMÈS, GUCCI, BALLANTYNE, CÉLINE, COURRÈGES, ESPRIT, BENETTON, LANVIN, VALENTINO, BURBERRYS, THE BODY SHOP, KENZO JUNGLE JAP, CERRUTTI 1881, MANDARINA DUCK, WATERFORD WEDGWOOD, BULGARI, MEISSEN, SHU UEMURA, TIMBERLAND, LOUIS VUITTON,** and many, many more.

THE LANDMARK, 16 Des Voeux Road Central, Hong Kong

▼

CENTRAL BUILDING: Next door to and occasionally adjoining The Landmark in some doorways, the Central Building is in the same tradition—without the fountains. In fact, it's hard to tell where one center stops and the other starts. The newness of the stores in the Central Building make it feel as if new life had been breathed into The Landmark. The space is not as large and therefore not as overwhelming; it's sort of the appetizer before the main course. More big names are here, of course, including **BASILE, CHARLES JOURDAN, PRADA, S. T. DUPONT, PIERRE BALMAIN, ZOE COSTE, BRUNO MAGLI, JUNKO SHIMADO, MAUD FRIZON CLUB,** and **LACOSTE.**

CENTRAL BUILDING, 19–23 Queen's Road Central, Hong Kong

▼

PRINCE'S BUILDING: This office building with five levels of shopping has so many big names now that it competes with The Landmark and the Central Building, both of which are across the street. The Prince's Building is easy to shop because it is perfectly square! It connects by bridge to the Mandarin Oriental Hotel (don't miss shopping there, either), and may be more fun than The Landmark for you. Among the many upscale tenants are **DIANE FREIS, CARTIER, FOGAL, ROYAL COPENHAGEN, CHANEL, ASCOT CHANG,** and **BREE** (Italian natural leather handbags). Then there's the useful category, such as **THE BANYAN TREE** (arts, crafts, home and table decor), **LAURA ASHLEY,** and trusty old **WATSON'S,** the drugstore that sells everything.

PRINCE'S BUILDING, Chater Road, Hong Kong

▼

MANDARIN ORIENTAL HOTEL SHOP-PING ARCADE: The glitziest stores in town fight to get space in the Mandarin Oriental Hotel, not only because the hotel is so fabulous and its clientele so tony, but because the location is prime. Part of your Central shopping spree must include a visit to the stores, which include **FERRAGAMO, KAI YIN LO, FENDI, DAVID'S SHIRTS, MAN HING CHEONG,** and **GEMSLAND.**

MANDARIN ORIENTAL HOTEL SHOPPING ARCADE, 5 Connaught Road Central, Hong Kong

▼

HARBOUR CITY: The shopping complex that occupies most of Tsim Sha Tsui's western shore has been combined under the name Harbour City. It includes Ocean Terminal, Ocean Centre, and Ocean Galleries along with Omni The Hong Kong Hotel, the Omni Marco Polo Hotel, and the Omni Prince Hotel. There are four levels of shopping from end to end, and if you can successfully negotiate your way from one end to the other, you won't even have to come up for air.

The idea of a shopping complex on the waterfront originated with **OCEAN TERMINAL,** which is the building that juts out into the water beside the Star Ferry Pier. As you come in to dock, you can't help seeing the big Toys "Я" Us sign on the bottom level. Ocean Terminal was so successful that Ocean Centre and then Ocean Galleries were developed. It is hard to tell one from the other unless you look at the distinguishing floor tiles. Ocean Terminal is the least claustrophobic part of the complex because there are windows. Once you get into the bowels of Ocean Centre and Ocean Galleries you need your compass and lots of luck to find your way back out.

Ocean Terminal has chic china shops like **ROYAL COPENHAGEN** and **HUNTER'S;** designer boutiques, including **DIANE FREIS, ALAIN MANOUKIAN,** and **BENETTON;** handicrafts shops, including **ARTS OF CHINA** and **MOUNTAIN FOLKCRAFT,** as well as lots of food shops. The entire basement is a children's specialty floor containing a **TOYS "Я" US** store and also furniture, clothing, and other baby-related shopping. There's even an optical shop that just sells children's eyeglasses frames. As you walk into Ocean Terminal stop at the information desk to pick up a complete listing of all the stores in Harbour City, along with the Harbour City map of Hong Kong. This map contains building locations that will help you get around town more easily.

OCEAN CENTRE is the next shopping complex as you walk away from the Star Ferry, followed by **OCEAN GALLERIES.** Although there are official lobbies, one seems to flow into the next, punctuated with a hotel along the way. The best hotel arcade in Harbour City is at the Omni The Hong Kong Hotel. There is a **JO-SEPH HO** shop on the main level and a mezzanine devoted to antiques shops. We must say that finding your way around Ocean Centre and Ocean Galleries can be confusing. The shops are in blocks and it is easy to get turned around looking for a number. We avoid coming here if there is a branch of the shop we want anywhere else. However, if it is raining, there is a typhoon, or the weather is so hot that you cannot breathe outside, Ocean Galleries and Ocean Centre start to look better. If you successfully make it to the far end, past the Omni Prince Hotel, treat yourself to some *dim sum* at Sun Tung Lok restaurant.

One stop farther up Canton Road is the **CHINA HONG KONG CITY** shopping complex. It is a major mall, with many fine, but ordinary, stores to browse in case you are not exhausted already.

HARBOUR CITY, 2 Canton Road, Kowloon

▼

PARK LANE SHOPPER'S BOULEVARD: This is a strip mall of unique architectural proportions that will certainly catch your eye (and maybe your credit card) as you stroll the infamous Nathan Road. The two-level mall has a park growing on its roof. It's made of white tile but broken up at intervals with quasi-Japanese *torii* in bright colors. About half of the space is occupied by **YUE HWA,** a Chinese department store making a rather upscale, modern, and Western debut in this branch store. There's also an **AMERICAN EXPRESS BANK** for changing traveler's checks (go upstairs).

PARK LANE SHOPPER'S BOULEVARD, Nathan Road, Kowloon

▼

THE PENINSULA HOTEL SHOPPING ARCADE: Cell-like shops in two wings of the hotel, with more on the mezzanine. The arcade hosts a number of big-name, high-ticket designers: **THE PEN BOUTIQUE, KENZO, LLADRÓ, GIEVES & HAWKES, LONGCHAMP, HERMÈS, POLO/RALPH LAUREN, TIFFANY, PRADA, CÉLINE, BELTRAMI, GENNY, NAF-NAF, GUCCI, MATSUDA, LÉONARD, GIANNI VERSACE, CARTIER, MCM, CHARLES JOURDAN,** etc. (We think the mezzanine's the best.)

THE PENINSULA HOTEL SHOPPING ARCADE, Salisbury Road, Kowloon

▼

KOWLOON HOTEL SHOPPING ARCADE: A small underground arcade you reach by escalator directly from the street. There are two levels of basement stores, all small but uncrowded. Who stays or shops here is beyond us. But if you do pop in, check out: **PRADA, HUNTER'S, CLAUDE MONTANA, ISSEY MIYAKE, TRUSSARDI, CRAIG'S,** and **NANCY MILLER.**

KOWLOON HOTEL SHOPPING ARCADE, 19–21 Nathan Road, Kowloon

▼

HYATT REGENCY HONG KONG SHOPPING ARCADE: A very fancy hotel in a prime shopping area, with stores including: **DUNHILL, LANVIN, CARLOS FALCHI, FRATELLI ROSSETTI, ZOE COSTE, ÉTIENNE AIGNER,** and our fave, **SHIRT STOP,** one of many branches of this discount house selling men's shirts and sweaters and some women's and unisex. When we were there last we scored a pile of gorgeous terrycloth bathrobes (unisex). This is pleasant shopping, right in the middle of the Golden Mile. The street-level back shops are not as nice as the front and basement shops.

HYATT REGENCY HONG KONG SHOPPING ARCADE, 67 Nathan Road, Kowloon

▼

CITYPLAZA: If you are in town for a very, very short time we don't suggest you visit Cityplaza and its various malls. But, if you are game for adventure, if you want to see how Chinese yuppies live, if you want a glance at housing "mansions" and an understanding of an entirely different aspect of Hong Kong living, then this is for you.

Travel takes a while on the MTR, but if you go in a hired car you'll get a magnificent view of Hong Kong Harbour and a tour of much of Victoria from your limo. Obviously, you're not going to spend the day here—but we do find it exhilarating. This is the kind of mall that has a multiplex cinema where the movies are in Chinese, not English. And that sums up the neighborhood. Don't forget while you're here that the newer and smaller Kornhill Plaza is out the back end of Cityplaza III.

Cityplaza is a pair of malls (Cityplaza II and III) that are the underpinnings to several highrise towers. There is a bridge between the two malls. Both are very American; this is where the upper-middle-class locals come to shop and get away from downtown and tourists.

There are levels and levels of stores, there's a food court, and there's a kiddie area called **WHIMSEYLAND,** with small rides for little ones. Cityplaza II is halfway filled with the many floors of **UNY,** a Japanese department store. There's also a supermarket, **MANNINGS** (like Watson's), **AMAZING GRACE** (crafts), and **WING ON** (a Chinese department store). Across the way at Cityplaza III is a multilevel **MARKS & SPENCER,** as well as the usual other shops and branch stores.

To round off the family feel, there's an ice-skating rink, bowling alley, and Rollerworld.

CITYPLAZA, 1111 King's Road, Quarry Bay, Hong Kong (MTR: Taikoo Shing)

▼

KORNHILL PLAZA: Located directly over the MTR station, Kornhill Plaza is not as big, as exciting, or as fancy as neighboring Cityplaza. There are two towers, north and south. North connects to Cityplaza; South has **JUSCO.** Jusco is a Japanese department store, and it has a fascinating supermarket on the lower level. This store has 250,000 square feet of shopping opportunities—the same size as a branch of Nordstrom's.

The beauty of being here isn't actually that you buy so much, but that you see so much; you absorb so much. This is the future of China. This is what success buys. If you care, don't miss it.

KORNHILL PLAZA, 2 Kornhill Road, Quarry Bay, Hong Kong (MTR: Taikoo Shing)

▼

TSIM SHA TSUI CENTRE: This city of hotels and shopping malls is not as educational or as exciting as the Cityplaza-Kornhill complex, but it's within walking distance of the Regent Hotel and Nathan Road, and therefore much more accessible.

Although there are a number of somewhat glamorous hotels here, including the highly rated Shangri-La, the area doesn't feel swank when you are out there (or in there) shopping. It feels very much like a "real people" part of town—and that's what's to recommend it, because it sure ain't gorgeous.

WING ON, the Chinese department store, has a large space at Wing On Plaza, the beginning of this city of shops. In TST Centre itself, there's **DIANE FREIS** and other not so well-known names. Farther back in another building is **ESPRIT,** with its own entrance. The various buildings often have their own names, from **TST CENTRE** to **HOUSTON CENTRE** to **AUTO CENTRE,** where Esprit is located.

TSIM SHA TSUI CENTRE, 62 Mody Road, Kowloon

▼

SWIRE HOUSE: We don't love Swire House as we once did (the American Express Bank has moved), but you can't beat the location in Central, between the Mandarin Oriental Hotel and The Landmark. The lobby floor does still have several big-name shops, and a few of the winners you may be looking for, like **BOTTEGA VENETA, DAKS, ISSEY MIYAKE, MOSCHINO, KENZO PARIS,** and **FILA.** The building has entrances on Connaught Road Central, Pedder Street, and Chater Road.

SWIRE HOUSE, Connaught Road Central, Hong Kong

▼

PEDDER BUILDING: We are going to be brutally honest about our feelings about the Pedder Building, with the understanding that no matter what we say, you're going to visit here anyway. (As well you should.)

The Pedder Building is not swank.

It's especially bad if you go in summer when the air is heavy and your feet are heavy and your shopping bags are heavy and the stores here are not too enlightening. But we digress. First, the facts:

The Pedder Building couldn't have a better location in all of Central.

The Pedder Building has several factory-outlet stores in it.

The Pedder Building could stand to be spruced up a little bit, which they happen to be doing now. There are several shops that are fancy, expensive, and not at all outlets—beware.

In the building, there are several adorable spaces (if you can stand to find them) including **DAVID SHEEKWAN** and **CHINA TEE CLUB** for lunch or tea. Outlets include **TAKPAC** (Anne Klein II), **LEATHER CONCEPTS, SHOPPER'S WORLD SAFARI,** and **WINTEX.**

Complain as we may about the building's decor, we do want to make it clear we had no trouble buying a knit dress for $20 and feeling good about it.

PEDDER BUILDING, 12 Pedder Street, Hong Kong

▼

ADMIRALTY SHOPPING CENTRE: We think Admiralty just plain missed the ferry. Although this is a major MTR stop and a great location, the stores here are mostly small-time local jobs for the population working in the surrounding buildings. Don't waste your time unless you are writing your dissertation on Hong Kong retail real estate.

ADMIRALTY SHOPPING CENTRE, Harcourt Road, Hong Kong (MTR: Admiralty)

▼

NEW WORLD SHOPPING CENTRE: We aren't wild for the New World Centre—to us it seems like more of the same old thing. But people who stay at the Regent Hotel or at the Sheraton love the New World Centre because it's almost out their bedroom door. The New World Shopping Centre is yet another massive multilevel, spic-and-span, concrete-and-cold-floor shopping center filled with little shops, one-hour photo stands, and ice cream vendors. It has one of the best air-conditioning systems in Hong Kong, which is important in summer, as well as a cute Japanese department store (**TOKYU**—open 10 A.M. to 9 P.M.; closed Thursday) on the street level. There are also **TOPPY** stores!

NEW WORLD SHOPPING CENTRE, 18–24 Salisbury Road, Kowloon

▼

SILVERCORD BUILDING: Located at the upper end of Tsim Sha Tsui, across from Harbour City, the Silvercord Building is best known for its sublevel shopping. If you're interested in computers, fax machines, or other high-tech electronic goodies, head straight to the basement, where the **EAST ASIA COMPUTER PLAZA** shops are located. It's a great place to begin your research before buying electronics. There is also a **CHINESE ARTS & CRAFTS STORE** that is big and fun (four floors), and if you can't find what you're looking for here, you can shop your way from Silvercord right to the harbor. Don't miss **LACE LANE**.

SILVERCORD BUILDING, Canton Road, Kowloon

▼

STAR HOUSE: Star House is the first building you come to upon exiting the Star Ferry and heading up Canton Road. You will see a

large branch of **CHINESE ARTS & CRAFTS STORE.**
The interesting shopping actually happens upstairs in the office building, where there are
some outlets such as **LEVANTE** (see page 194)
and specialty stores like **NAG TRADE LIMITED**
(see page 195). Don't let the tacky 1st-floor
arcade turn you away.

STAR HOUSE, Canton Road, Kowloon

Japanese Department Stores

J apanese department stores must be considered the eighth wonder of the world. They
are so total, so complete, so very stagger-
ing in their stock that it's almost overwhelming. Visitors to Japan often go nowhere
else but department stores. Visitors to Hong
Kong should take some time for a few of these
stores just to see what they are like, if not to
buy anything.

Basically, Japanese department stores in foreign (foreign to Japan) countries are there to
serve Japanese expats. The Japanese department stores in London sell the same things
Harrods does; the ones in Hong Kong sell a
little of everything. If you expect just Japanese
merchandise, you are very, very wrong. Every
big-name French and Italian designer is represented in the bigger Japanese department stores.
Japanese cosmetics (fabulous) are sold in quan-
tities; and selection of all types of products is
maximal. Causeway Bay has several Japanese
department stores right near each other, so
you may want to check a few of them out
while you are there.

Prices in department stores tend to be high,
and we don't buy a lot here; we just drool.

One final word to claustrophobics: Don't go
during rush hours. Stores are open until 9 or

10 P.M., so relax and enjoy yourself away from the madding crowd.

DAIMARU: Closed on Wednesday in the traditional Japanese habit of closing one day a week, Daimaru is fun and known to us for its clean, well-marked toilets, which we use when in the neighborhood. Asian pop music blares and major designer goods are abundant. Prices are not bargain-basement but are no higher than at other Japanese department stores.

Daimaru is divided into two large department stores, one for fashions and one for housewares and furniture. The stores feel much more Japanese than the other department stores. This is a good "real people" resource if you live in Hong Kong.

Inexpensive Japanese (a fashion style you will grow to appreciate when you see it) is cute and fun—great for teens. There are watches and pearls here, but the selection and quality are not as snazzy as at Mitsukoshi. Daimaru is more middle-class than some of the other stores; the real buys here are in Japanese fashions. Hours are 10:30 A.M. to 9:30 P.M.

DAIMARU, Fashion Square, Paterson Street, Hong Kong (MTR: Causeway Bay)

▼

ISETAN: Isetan is more young at heart than the other Japanese department stores. It's a smaller store, across the street from the Regent, and offers a small hint of Japanese taste. This store also has several basement levels, but is not attached to an MTR station. Fun for teens; convenient enough to your basic Kowloon shopping spree that you can pop in for a few minutes. Hours: Daily, 10 A.M. to 9 P.M.

ISETAN, Sheraton Hotel Shopping Arcade, Salisbury Road, Kowloon

MATSUZAKAYA: This department store closes on Thursday, but otherwise it's open from 10:30 A.M. to 9:30 P.M. It feels a lot like Sears but has pockets of designer clothes here and there. If you crave Godiva chocolates, you can buy them here. The ground floor has cosmetics, perfumes, handbags, and accessories; the 1st floor is ladies' and children's ready-to-wear; the 2nd floor is men's and sports; and the 3rd floor is housewares, stationery, and toys.

The overall quality is everyday Hong Kong, which probably is not your look back in the United States. Display of fashion is not good, and we aren't wild for the store—except for its good cosmetics department and those marvelous Godiva chocolates.

MATSUZAKAYA, Paterson Street, Hong Kong
   (MTR: Causeway Bay)

▼

MITSUKOSHI: There are now two branch stores of Mitsukoshi in Hong Kong, one on each side of the harbor. Mitsukoshi can be appreciated even before you set foot in the actual store. Occupying most of the ground floor of the marbled Hennessy Centre, it is one of the largest and fanciest of the Japanese department stores in Causeway Bay. Just looking at it is exciting. Fine watches, pearls, leather handbags, and some designer labels dot the ground-floor display cases. Compared to other Japanese department stores, Mitsukoshi is one of the most lovely and elegant—especially on the main floor. Prices here are Japanese standard, which means there are no bargains.

As you descend into the guts of the store, each floor gets less and less American. The lower-level fashions downstairs are geared more for Hong Kong taste and budget. As you go down, the lights get brighter and the music seems louder. Don't go if you have a headache.

Mitsukoshi has designer clothes and accessories—Gucci, Lanvin, Christian Dior, Guy Laroche, Chloé, Mila Schön, etc. The housewares department is great fun; there is also a grocery store on B3. Hours are Sunday through Friday, 10 A.M. to 9 P.M., and Saturday till 9:30 P.M. (closed Tuesday).

Mitsukoshi Kowloon is across from Harbour City at the high end, closer to Silvercord, and takes up much of a block and leads into a mall that is part of the Ramada Renaissance Hotel. Speaking of renaissances, this whole block and the surrounding area has been building and building and growing to house a number of big stores, so Mitsukoshi actually brought a boom with it.

The store is big and modern, with a nice kids' department downstairs where your children can play and test Nintendo games to their hearts' delight. This is where you can buy the transformer that will allow you to play a Japanese-style Nintendo game on your child's American Nintendo. The plastic transformer costs about $8.

MITSUKOSHI
Kowloon Sun Plaza Arcade, 28 Canton Road, Kowloon

Hennessy Centre, 500 Hennessy Road, Hong Kong (MTR: Causeway Bay)

▼

SEIBU: Remember the old days when Bloomingdale's really was something special? Seibu is that store. We honestly believe they took everything Bloomie's had to offer and then made it better. Locals complain that the store is as expensive as Lane Crawford. Surely Seibu considers Lane Crawford the competition, instead of the other Japanese department stores.

Seibu has fabulous stores in Tokyo (and all of Japan) and now offers Hong Kong its upscale lifestyle and fashion. The store here is no larger than Lane Crawford (far smaller than the one on the Ginza), but it gives you a fine taste of what retailing refinement can be. There are no bargains, however.

SEIBU, The Mall at Pacific Place, 88 Queensway, Hong Kong (MTR: Admiralty)

▼

SOGO: Sogo is right over the Causeway Bay MTR station, which makes it very convenient. (Or, if you are driving, there is free parking for two hours at Windsor House.) Sogo is open daily from 10:30 A.M. to 10 P.M., so you can get in some nighttime shopping with pleasure. All the big designers are represented here. Prices are good on Japanese designers, such as Hiroko Koshino, whom we have been buying in Milan or at Alma in New York.

Sogo plays recognizable Muzak as you zip up and down escalators—designers on the ground floor; ladies' fashions, cosmetics, and shoes on B1; food on B2. There are more ladies' fashions on floors 1 and 2; don't miss the cosmetics bar on the 1st floor; men's fashions are on 3; 4 is sports and hi-fi equipment; 5 is household goods and furniture; 6 has babies' and maternity items; and 7 offers stationery. On the 1st floor there's an adorable "Café City" decorated in pink-and-black Art Deco and ready to convince you that you aren't in Hong Kong. Sogo claims to be the world's largest department store; their branches in Japan are to die for.

SOGO, Lockhart Road, Hong Kong (MTR: Causeway Bay)

British Department Stores

I t seems perfectly normal for there to be British department stores in a British crown colony—especially one that was set up for the sole purpose of trade—but we are sorely disappointed that Harrods doesn't have an outlet in Hong Kong.

LANE CRAWFORD: Lane Crawford is the most prestigious Western-style department store in Hong Kong, and a jewel to those who work and live here but who crave the elegance of Old World charm in a retail setting. Lane Crawford is not huge by American standards, but it's large enough to give comfort and to offer the leading brands of merchandise. It is not really there for tourists, but it does offer the guarantee that you are not getting fakes, seconds, or inferior merchandise. Snobs often like to buy their jewelry here.

Lane Crawford was created as a full-service English department store for the people who live here. It doesn't have the food halls of Harrods or the young-working-girl selection of Selfridge's, but it does offer cradle-to-grave services along with the merchandise. The name has snob appeal in Hong Kong, with a ranking as high as Neiman Marcus in the U.S.

We have never seen anything in Lane Crawford we didn't see anywhere else, and find the store worthwhile only if you seek to escape the realities of Hong Kong (and many do . . . if only for an hour), or want to see a lot of merchandise in a manner you can deal with—as opposed to the wretched excesses elsewhere in Hong Kong.

LANE CRAWFORD

Lane Crawford House, Queen's Road Central, Hong Kong

74 Nathan Road, Kowloon

The Mall at Pacific Place, 88 Queensway, Hong Kong (MTR: Admiralty)

MARKS & SPENCER: M&S has come to Hong Kong, and in a big way. Every place you turn (especially in the malls) you spot a new one. Dodwell stores have been absorbed into M&S and then new M&S's have sprouted. Yippee skippee—a chance to buy more St. Michael's underwear.

Now then. As much as we love M&S, we admit that there are no great Hong Kong bargains here. Being in the store, especially the grocery department, is just like being in England. Right down to the prices. What you are paying for is the M&S reputation for quality and value; but we are not talking factory-outlet prices.

MARKS & SPENCER, Harbour City/Ocean Galleries, 25–27 Canton Road, Kowloon

Chinese Department Stores

There are several Chinese department stores in Hong Kong, but few of them are glamorous. They are a real experience to shop, are a fine source of visual treats, and very often have some bargains.

CHINESE ARTS & CRAFTS STORE: This store is shocking to most Americans because it is elegant. (There are several branches, the biggest one being in Wanchai, but all are very nice.) Stores are open every day of the week, including Sunday. Locals sometimes call this store by its initials: CAC.

Each shop is slightly different, but most of the merchandise is the same. *One warning:* The shops are meant to bring cash into the Communist Chinese government. To make the most, the most is asked. These stores happen to be very expensive, for what they are selling. By American standards, the prices are good. By local standards, they are outrageously high.

The silk fabric (yardgoods) department is fun, although the prices are cheaper in Jardine's or the Lanes. We love the porcelain, baskets, and tablecloths. We've been told by those who know that this is a reputable place to buy jade. There's no imitation passed off as real here. Be warned, however: Real jade is quite pricey. The store will ship for you; sales help have been very pleasant to us. A good place for souvenirs. This is the most Western of the various Chinese department stores. Hours in all stores are basically Monday to Saturday, 10 A.M. to 6:30 P.M.; some stores may be open on Sunday. The Wanchai branch is convenient to the new convention center.

CHINESE ARTS & CRAFTS STORES (H.K.) LTD.
Shell House, Queen's Road Central, Hong Kong

Silvercord Building, Canton Road, Kowloon

China Resources Building, 26 Harbour Road, Hong Kong (MTR: Wanchai)

▼

WING ON: Wing On has Western-style merchandise at about one quarter the U.S. price. Many prices are lower than at Stanley Market. We're not talking Calvin Klein, but you can find some inexpensive work clothes here. Large-size Americans need not apply. This store was really a shocker in that it offered so much. Needless to say, there are not a lot of tourists here. Avoid weekend shopping. It's very crowded at all branches.

WING ON
361 Nathan Road, Kowloon (MTR: Yau Ma Tei)

26 Des Voeux Road Central, Hong Kong

62 Mody Road, Kowloon

YUE HWA: If you can't make it all the way to China, stop by here for a taste of the real thing. If you need acupuncture needles, stop by the counter on the 1st floor. (Promise her anything, but give her acupuncture needles. . . .) The main store is rather jam-packed and junky, but the newer Park Lane store is almost as nice as Macy's. Ignore the Western goods and buy Chinese. They mail to the U.S. Hours are daily from 9:30 or 10 A.M. to 8 or 9 P.M.

YUE HWA

Main store, 301–9 Nathan Road, Kowloon (MTR: Yau Ma Tei)

Park Lane Shopper's Boulevard, 151 Nathan Road, Kowloon

Basement store, 54–64 Nathan Road, Kowloon

▼

SHUI HING CO. LTD.: We mention this Chinese department store because we like it. We like it because it makes us laugh. Very few Chinese stores understand the Western concept of fashion or style. However, this store is on to it. When you approach the store on a rainy day, there is a basket filled with plastic umbrella shields for you to choose from. We've only seen this done elsewhere in Fendi. When you get to the handbag section where the cheap copies of good bags are, you'll find the only plastic copies of Paloma Picasso's handbags you may find anywhere in the world. Furthermore, the store is located right in the heart of downtown Kowloon, so you'll automatically pass by when you prowl Nathan Road.

SHUI HING CO. LTD., 23–26 Nathan Road, Kowloon

▼

CHUNG KIU CHINESE PRODUCTS EMPORIUM: Since you already know we are fond of Chinese department stores, let us now say this is one of our faves. The sales help is usually rude. The visual stimulation in the store is nil. The prices are high when compared to the street. And yet it is packed with things we like to look at, and we consider it a valuable resource for Chinese arts and crafts. We've bought many a souvenir here as well.

The store locations make it a must; two are deep in "real people" Kowloon, and one is right under a factory-outlet building in downtown Kowloon.

CHUNG KIU CHINESE PRODUCTS EMPORIUM
Sands Building, 17 Hankow Road, Kowloon
528–32 Nathan Road, Kowloon (MTR: Yau Ma Tei)
47–51 Shan Tung Road, Kowloon (MTR: Mong Kok)

Continental Big Names

GIORGIO ARMANI/EMPORIO ARMANI: These expensive duds are strictly for the local rich guys. Even the stores are not as drop-dead gorgeous as in Europe. The Emporio store in Kowloon is actually small; the Central shop is much nicer. For even higher prices, see regular Armani in The Landmark, where the truly rich shop.

GIORGIO ARMANI
The Landmark, Gloucester Tower, 16 Des Voeux Road Central, Hong Kong
Mandarin Oriental Hotel, 5 Connaught Road Central, Hong Kong

EMPORIO ARMANI
Harbour City/Ocean Centre, 5 Canton Road, Kowloon
16 Queen's Road Central, Hong Kong

▼

BALLANTYNE: Sweaters, sweaters, and more sweaters at prices that will send you right to Marks & Spencer.

BALLANTYNE
> The Landmark, Gloucester Tower, 16 Des Voeux Road Central, Hong Kong
> The Mall at Pacific Place, 88 Queensway, Hong Kong (MTR: Admiralty)

▼

BALLY: Bally has a great line of shoes and sportswear. We buy it in Europe, in the United States, and yes, even in Hong Kong. The shop's interior is the latest in high-tech, neoclassic design. The prices are good, although no steal. Best of all, the shoes are comfortable and easy to walk in—essential for Hong Kong. Bally has many boutiques to choose from, including those found in large department stores.

BALLY
> The Peninsula Hotel, Salisbury Road, Kowloon
> The Landmark, Gloucester Tower, 16 Des Voeux Road Central, Hong Kong

▼

BOTTEGA VENETA: Bottega Veneta is the *crème de la crème* of leathergoods, even in Hong Kong where leather handbags are produced with abandon. We have seen copies of Chanel that could pass muster, but if you want Bottega, you have to pay the price. The shiny ground-floor boutique in Swire House has a terrific selection. It is cheaper to buy Bottega in Italy or during a good sale at Neiman Marcus.

BOTTEGA VENETA, Swire House (ground floor), Connaught Road Central, Hong Kong

▼

CACHAREL: If you love the soft, elegant look of Jean Cacharel's clothing for children and young adults, you will be very happy here. The main shop in The Landmark is all blond wood, which makes it look more spacious than it is. The clothing is artfully arranged around the perimeter by style. There are lots of selections up to age 6. The baby clothing is the best.

CACHAREL

The Landmark, 16 Des Voeux Road Central, Hong Kong

Harbour City/Ocean Centre, 5 Canton Road, Kowloon

▼

CARTIER: Cartier has a number of boutiques in Hong Kong. We have observed over the years that those who go in to buy usually come out smiling. A gold Cartier watch costs $6,000 and up. Cartier also makes a very nice scarf for under $200, and purses for under $500. Other stores are licensed to sell Cartier goods, so shop around. For the most part prices are similar all over town.

CARTIER

Prince's Building (ground floor), Chater Road, Hong Kong

The Peninsula Hotel, Salisbury Road, Kowloon

▼

CÉLINE: Céline is very popular in Hong Kong. It is not as showy as Chanel, or as expensive as Hermès, but has a classic look that coordinates with dressier and casual clothing alike. There are several boutiques located in the main shopping areas of Hong Kong and Kowloon, each with its own mix of pieces. The boutiques in the Sogo and Tokyu department stores are less formal, and the merchandise is more casual.

CÉLINE

The Landmark, Gloucester Tower, 16 Des Voeux Road Central, Hong Kong

The Peninsula Hotel, Salisbury Road, Kowloon

▼

CHANEL: We have good news. There are many Chanel boutiques in Hong Kong, and they are not empty. Since Karl Lagerfeld began designing the line, it has been walking out of the stores in the United States and Europe. The new Hong Kong boutiques increase your chance of finding something you love.

Prices are comparable to those in the United States. A nice pair of daytime earrings will cost $150–$200. Necklaces run $250–$500 depending on their intricacy. The quilted handbags start at $650 and go up. Those who want Chanel don't seem to mind paying the prices.

CHANEL

Prince's Building, Chater Road, Hong Kong

The Peninsula Hotel, Salisbury Road, Kowloon

The Regent Hotel, Salisbury Road, Kowloon

▼

COURRÈGES: Courrèges boutiques provide simple, white backdrops for the colorful structured clothing that you have to be in good shape to wear. We still think of the '70s when we see the styling, but not everybody does, or they wouldn't be selling so well. The skiwear is especially appealing.

COURRÈGES

The Landmark, Gloucester Tower, 16 Des Voeux Road Central, Hong Kong

Harbour City/Ocean Centre, 5 Canton Road, Kowloon

CHRISTIAN DIOR: Once exclusively a high-end line, Christian Dior now caters to those with good taste but a more modest pocketbook. Everything you might need, from shoes to shirts to perfume and jewelry, is available. We have seen a lot of Christian Dior labels at various factory outlets over the years, and suspect that some of it is made right in Hong Kong. Christian Dior Monsieur caters just to the guys.

CHRISTIAN DIOR
> The Landmark, Edinburgh Tower, 16 Des Voeux Road Central, Hong Kong
> The Peninsula Hotel, Salisbury Road, Kowloon

CHRISTIAN DIOR MONSIEUR
> Prince's Building, Chater Road, Hong Kong

▼

ZOE COSTE: We first fell in love with Zoe Coste's jewelry creations in Cannes and Juan-les-Pins, France. Her look is sort of Egyptian/Greek princess. Prices are high, but we love to go in, try on, and pretend. There are Zoe Coste shops in New York, Chicago, Miami, and Houston as well as in Monte Carlo, Geneva, and Paris.

ZOE COSTE
> Hyatt Regency Hong Kong, 67 Nathan Road, Kowloon
> Shell House, Queen's Road Central, Hong Kong

▼

DAKS: A relative newcomer to the Hong Kong fashion scene, Daks is British to the core. If you need those regimental ties, brass-buttoned blazers, or serious walking-pants trousers, Daks will fit the bill. If you are looking for Continental pizzazz, this is not your store.

DAKS

Prince's Building, Chater Road, Hong Kong
The Peninsula Hotel, Salisbury Road, Kowloon

▼

ALFRED DUNHILL: For the man who must look British, preppy, rich, and casual—all at once.

ALFRED DUNHILL

The Peninsula Hotel, Salisbury Road, Kowloon
Hyatt Regency Hong Kong, 67 Nathan Road, Kowloon
Prince's Building, Chater Road, Hong Kong
The Mall at Pacific Place (Level 3), 88 Queensway, Hong Kong (MTR: Admiralty)

▼

ESCADA: The Escada boutique is a temple to what money can buy and what good design is all about. From the time you walk in the door you are hit with splashes of color emanating from the floor and rack displays. Choices are overwhelming. Prices are high. This West German line is very popular in the United States and Canada, but we did not see a lot of crossover merchandise. While you are there, take a look at the slightly less expensive Crisca and Laurèl lines.

ESCADA

Wheelock House, Pedder Street, Hong Kong
China Hong Kong City, Kowloon

▼

FENDI: Ouch! When you see the Fendi prices you might consider it cheaper to book a ticket to Italy. We love this line and buy it extensively in Rome, where prices are reasonable. However, Fendi's Hong Kong stores offer no bargains. If you are dying for those little FFFFFs, buy a key case.

FENDI
> Hankow Centre, Ashley Road, Kowloon
> Mandarin Oriental Hotel, 5 Connaught Road Central, Hong Kong

▼

FERRAGAMO: The shoes cost 25% more than they do in the U.S., and not every store stocks the wide range of sizes that the brand is famous for. In addition to their freestanding boutiques you'll find Ferragamo in Lane Crawford and Matsuzakaya.

FERRAGAMO
> The Regent Hotel, Salisbury Road, Kowloon
> Mandarin Oriental Hotel, 5 Connaught Road Central, Hong Kong
> The Peninsula Hotel, Salisbury Road, Kowloon

▼

JEAN-PAUL GAULTIER: A great-looking shop combined with great-looking clothing will attract our attention anytime. Gaultier has both in his Prince's Building boutique. The decor is reminiscent of a submarine, with the racks finished in a tarnished green brass veneer, and portholes for lights. The clothing is as wonderful as the decor, although Gaultier is no longer considered so weird by design standards.

JEAN-PAUL GAULTIER
> Prince's Building, Chater Road, Hong Kong
> Harbour City/Ocean Centre, 5 Canton Road, Kowloon

GIVENCHY: Audrey Hepburn looks great in Givenchy. We love the shop and can imagine her in all the clothes. In the last few years, the men's clothing has become even more popular. As a matter of fact, the Hong Kong Givenchy boutiques consider the menswear their best-selling line.

GIVENCHY, The Landmark, Gloucester Tower, 16 Des Voeux Road Central, Hong Kong

▼

GUCCI: The big Gucci shop in Hong Kong is in a corner of The Landmark. It is not visible from the main atrium, but it does have street windows on Des Voeux Road Central. We happen to like the scarves, but find all of the GGs on the doors and mirrors amusing. The Peninsula Hotel has a more tasteful boutique, as do several department stores and malls.

GUCCI

The Landmark, Gloucester Tower, 16 Des Voeux Road Central, Hong Kong
The Peninsula Hotel, Salisbury Road, Kowloon
109 Repulse Bay, Hong Kong (take a taxi)

▼

HERMÈS: The main entrance to Hermès, in The Landmark, is on the street, so do not be misled by the little showcase window you see across from Gucci. Walk outside and into the real shop. This is our favorite Hermès outside of Paris. Although the prices are not as good, the selection is very fine indeed. If you are dying for Hermès bath towels, jewelry, belts, purses, ashtrays, bathing suits, sweaters, or scarves, you will be a happy person. You may be able to find the scarf for slightly less in your airline duty-free selections.

HERMÈS

The Landmark, Gloucester Tower, 16 Des Voeux Road Central, Hong Kong

The Peninsula Hotel, Salisbury Road, Kowloon

▼

IKEA: Swedish knockdown furniture and modern home-furnishing touches with contemporary flair, at prices that are exactly the same as at the Ikea near you (if there is one). While they have some good ideas, this isn't what you came to Hong Kong to buy, is it?

IKEA, Sun Plaza Arcade, 28 Canton Road, Kowloon

▼

KARL LAGERFELD: Despite the fact that everywhere you turn in Hong Kong is a copy of a Lagerfeld-designed Chanel suit, this is the real Lagerfeld line that is made in Italy. Daring and divine but oh, so pricey.

KARL LAGERFELD, The Landmark, Edinburgh Tower, 16 Des Voeux Road Central, Hong Kong

▼

LANVIN: One of the oldest French houses, Lanvin is famous for fashion and for fragrance. My Sin and Arpège have been top brands ever since we could sniff. The classic, conservative clothing has become more popular with the fashionable young in the last few years. Lanvin's shop in The Landmark, located next to the fountain, is all cream-and-black decor. A center circular display holds the handbags and accessories; silk shirts, suits, and other ready-to-wear pieces are displayed along the walls. The choices are conservative; the prices are high.

LANVIN

> The Landmark, Gloucester Tower, 16 Des Voeux Road Central, Hong Kong
>
> Hyatt Regency Hong Kong, 67 Nathan Road, Kowloon

▼

CLAUDE MONTANA: Claude Montana makes the clothes that we diet to wear. You must be tall and thin to look right in them, but when you do, everyone turns around. All his shops are classically simple, and allow the designs to stand on their own. The two shops in Central and Kowloon are no exception.

CLAUDE MONTANA

> The Landmark, Edinburgh Tower, 16 Des Voeux Road Central, Hong Kong
>
> Kowloon Hotel, 19–21 Nathan Road, Kowloon

▼

MOSCHINO: An itsy-bitsy teeny-weeny shop with the great clothes but not the wit for windows or interior design. For locals who must be seen in these Italian-made duds. This is a wonderful designer who is not getting his just deserts with this so-so store.

MOSCHINO, Swire House, Connaught Road Central, Hong Kong

▼

NINA RICCI: Nina Ricci has made a significant dent in Hong Kong retailing by offering great accessories that complement any outfit. Prices are moderate for designer goods. When we were there a pair of sunglasses was $75. Ties cost $50.

NINA RICCI
The Peninsula Hotel, Salisbury Road, Kowloon

The Regent Hotel, Salisbury Road, Kowloon

▼

TRUSSARDI: The Italian Trussardi family is becoming a strong presence in the Hong Kong market. In the years we have been visiting the boutiques here and abroad, we have seen a tremendous growth in both the quality and the quantity of the lines offered. You can now outfit the whole family in regular Trussardi, Trussardi Jeans, or Trussardi Junior.

TRUSSARDI
The Peninsula Hotel, Salisbury Road, Kowloon

Harbour City/Ocean Centre, 5 Canton Road, Kowloon

▼

GIANNI VERSACE: Another Italian master for those who can afford his quasi-architectural splendor and fine color style, mixed with a smart trace of humor.

GIANNI VERSACE
Kowloon Hotel, 19–21 Nathan Road, Kowloon

The Landmark, Gloucester Tower, 16 Des Voeux Road Central, Hong Kong

The Peninsula Hotel, Salisbury Road, Kowloon

▼

LOUIS VUITTON: Louis Vuitton has a street entrance, while officially being in The Landmark. This particular Vuitton reminds us of a mini Paris store, with the emphasis on the decor matching the luggage. However, the range of merchandise is petite by comparison. Prices are similar to those in Paris, and better than in the United States in most cases. This store is incredibly popular with tourists and is usually jammed with customers. Know your merchandise before you come. The street-market imitations have been cleared out, so don't expect to beat the system this time.

LOUIS VUITTON

The Landmark, Gloucester Tower, 16 Des Voeux Road Central, Hong Kong

The Peninsula Hotel, Salisbury Road, Kowloon

Repulse Bay Shopping Arcade, Hong Kong (take a taxi)

The Regent Hotel, Salisbury Road, Kowloon

American Big Names

ESPRIT: The market in casual American clothing has been captured by Esprit. Stores are all over town. Some are big and fancy (Causeway Bay and Tsim Sha Tsui East), others comfortable and fun. We love the clothing, but don't feel that it is any special deal in Hong Kong.

ESPRIT

88 Hing Fat Street, Causeway Bay, Hong Kong (MTR: Causeway Bay)

Auto Plaza, 65 Mody Road, Kowloon

Park Lane Shopper's Boulevard, Nathan Road, Kowloon

Cityplaza, Taikoo Shing, Quarry Bay, Hong Kong (MTR: Taikoo Shing)

▼

DIANE FREIS: Diane Freis is, without doubt, the most famous designer in Hong Kong. Originally from California, Freis was on a trip to

Hong Kong in the early '70s and decided to stay. She began designing the basic Freis dress—a panoply of three coordinating prints—and sold it through local stores. She was an instant smash with local-ladies-of-wealth, and soon had her own company.

Although she now runs a multimillion-dollar company, her basic design philosophy is still the same, although Freis continues to modify and update her styles. She oversees or personally creates every design that comes out of her factory.

Because Freis lives and works in Hong Kong, she sells a large percentage of her clothes from her boutiques. She does not believe in sales, and just recently was urged to open a factory outlet to handle merchandise from the previous season's line. Since Diane Freis dresses are timeless and travel without a wrinkle (we have put them to the test), we know that even last season's merchandise won't look like last season.

A Diane Freis original sells at Neiman Marcus for from $400 up, but in Hong Kong you can buy them for from $280 up. There is quite a savings, even buying retail.

One warning: There are Freis imitations sold under other names. Do not be misled. A Diane Freis dress has a label that says so; the fabric has her signature in the design.

DIANE FREIS

Prince's Building, Chater Road, Hong Kong
Harbour City/Ocean Terminal, Canton Road, Kowloon
The Regent Hotel, Salisbury Road, Kowloon
The Mall at Pacific Place, 88 Queensway, Hong Kong (MTR: Admiralty)

▼

POLO/RALPH LAUREN: We have been tracking Mr. Lauren for years, in hopes of finding a factory outlet. We finally did find one in Puerto Rico, which doesn't help if you are in Hong Kong. Until we find the factory, his shops are the best locations to pick up men's, women's, and children's clothing. It is not nearly so complete a selection as you will find in New York or Los Angeles, but what you find are good solid basics. We have found the prices to be slightly better than in the United States, but they are still very high, no bargains in the stores at all. There are both Polo/Ralph Lauren boutiques and Ralph Lauren for Women boutiques, in most cases they are next door to each other or nearby.

RALPH LAUREN and **POLO/RALPH LAUREN**
Central Building, 19–23 Queen's Road Central, Hong Kong
The Peninsula Hotel, Salisbury Road, Kowloon

▼

TIFFANY & CO.: If you want breakfast at Tiffany & Co., you may stop by—otherwise consider this a local source for prestige plus. Nothing is inexpensive.

TIFFANY & CO.
The Peninsula Hotel, Salisbury Road, Kowloon
The Landmarks (street level), 16 Des Voeux Road Central, Hong Kong

▼

TOYS "Я" US: You can't miss the sign while you are on the Star Ferry; your kids will insist this is one of their first stops in town. Even they will be disappointed. This is not the world's largest toy store; we don't care what the ads say. No price breaks that impress us. Not even a selection that impresses us. Every now and then you'll find line extensions that don't exist in the U.S., but this is not going to be the thrill you were hoping for.

TOYS ''Я'' US, Harbour City/Ocean Terminal, Canton Road, Kowloon

Asian Big Names

KENZO: We are really cheating by putting Kenzo Takada under Asian Big Names. Yes, he is Japanese, but more French than anything else. His clothing originates in Paris, and it is wonderful. Kenzo's new store in Swire House carries a good selection of his line.

KENZO, Swire House, Connaught Road Central, Hong Kong

▼

TOKIO KUMAGAI: If you are a fan of original Maud Frizon designs, or of any shoes that are wacky and fun, then Tokio Kumagai shoes will make you smile. There are shoes with faces, feathers, and pigtails. Mr. Kumagai has died, but a design staff is carrying out his concepts. We also liked the ties and leather accessories. The men's shoes are made in Italy and look sturdy enough to last for years.

TOKIO KUMAGAI
Swire House, Connaught Road Central, Hong Kong
The Peninsula Hotel, Salisbury Road, Kowloon

▼

MATSUDA: Matsuda is one of our favorite Japanese designers. The clothing is architectural and distinctive. The prices are high, and you may be able to do better at a big sale in the United States. The interior of the store is a work of art and worth stopping by to see.

MATSUDA, Swire House, Connaught Road Central, Hong Kong

▼

ISSEY MIYAKE: One of the premier architects of Japanese spare fashion, Miyake appeals to a select few. You have to have a certain flair to wear the designs well. If you're one of these fashionable few, you'll want to head immediately to the Miyake and Plantation shops in Swire House. None of his stores (even in Tokyo) carry a lot of stock, so putting together a wardrobe can be a frustrating job. The Plantation line is less expensive, but by no means cheap.

ISSEY MIYAKE, Swire House, Connaught Road Central, Hong Kong
ISSEY MIYAKE PERMANENTE, The Landmark, Gloucester Tower, 16 Des Voeux Road Central, Hong Kong

Local Big Names

Since we first began traveling to Hong Kong, the Hong Kong designers have been increasingly in the international spotlight. Local designers like Kai Yin Lo and Joseph Ho have been moving successfully on to the international scene as well. We find fashions by these hot local designers to be among the best buys in Hong Kong. Their designs will often cost less in Hong Kong than in the United States or Europe. There is usually not any crossover with the merchandise in the U.S. stores. For instance, Diane Freis designs are not done in bulk, and Kai Yin Lo specializes in one-of-a-kind jewelry.

The Hong Kong Trade Development Council sponsors "Fashion Week" every January, during which buyers come to Hong Kong to see what is new in manufacturing and what the hot talent is designing. Many previously unknown designers have had their start this way. Some of them are now well established, and a new crop of "young" designers are following in their footsteps.

Caveat: You may know of a designer with a Chinese name and assume his or her clothes are cheaper in Hong Kong. This is not necessarily true. After all, there are many American or Canadian designers with Asian surnames who may not even manufacture in Hong Kong—for instance, Joanie Char, Flora Kung, and Alfred Sung.

All the locals mentioned design Western-style garments in Western sizes.

NANCY MILLER: First in the furniture business in Hong Kong, Korean-born Miller has a successful business mostly in imported Korean chests, but has branched out to take over the area vacated when Jenny Lewis went out of business. That means Miller makes very dressy clothes and takes advantage of local beading and embroidery skills to bring in the glitz look for a price you can't touch at home. We aren't knocked out, but someone must be.

NANCY MILLER, Kowloon Hotel, 19–21 Nathan Road, Kowloon

▼

DFS: There is a small retailing war going on in Hong Kong, and the victors appear to be the people who own Duty Free Shoppers (known as DFS), a set of stores with branches in Kowloon, Macao, and the airport. We're not privy to the details, but the rumor is something to the effect that these guys lowered prices to beat airport duty-free prices and were undercutting the airport shopping scene, so they were invited to the airport in order to stabilize prices. Now their in-town prices and the airport prices are the same.

Anyway, think about a huge airport duty-free shop, and you get the picture as to what these guys have for sale. Please note that cosmetics now have duty on them in Hong Kong. Also note that DFS has the duty-free shops in San Francisco's international terminal, and that prices are the same.

D F S
Hankow Centre, 15 Hankow Road, Kowloon
Chinachem, 77 Mody Road, Kowloon

▼

JOSEPH HO: We can't quite figure out Ho; he has numerous lines ranging from Studio to Signatures to J. Ho to Joseph Ho, and they all seem to be slightly different. This guy is doing more than Calvin Klein. There are now two outlets to unload all the goodies. The upstairs one in the Winner Building is more outlet-style; the one at street level across the street under Kaiser Estates Phase II is as lovely as any store in Central. Go figure.

JOSEPH HO, The Regent Hotel Shopping Arcade, Salisbury Road, Kowloon
JOSEPH HO OUTLET, 36 Man Yue Street, Hung Hom, Kowloon

▼

RAGENCE LAM: Ragence Lam attended London's Harrow School of Art and Royal College of Art, after which he came back to Hong Kong long enough to win the first Young Designer Award (1977) from the Hong Kong

Trade Development Council. He continued to work out of London until 1980, when he returned to Hong Kong on a full-time basis. He is no longer considered new, but is definitely a local big name. He now operates both a retail and a wholesale business, with a factory in Hong Kong and a beautiful boutique in Central. His reputation is for fabulous, verging on way-out, designs. If you dress to be noticed and want to buy a designer on the way up, make sure you visit the modern and lush boutique. The shop is simply called Ragence.

RAGENCE LAM, Swire House, Connaught Road Central, Hong Kong

▼

EDDIE LAU: Lau started in the fashion business at the age of 11, learning the tailoring trade. By the age of 14 he owned his own shop. Not satisfied, Lau went to study at the St. Martin School of Art in London, learning style along with technique. He has been designing and manufacturing in Hong Kong for over ten years now, and is one of the top talents in the field. His work is colorful, expensive, and exciting, but not as visible as it was years ago. The C.A.C. stores do have boutiques for this artist.

EDDIE LAU
Mandarin Oriental Hotel, 5 Connaught Road Central, Hong Kong
Chinese Arts & Crafts Stores (H.K.) Ltd., Silvercord Building, Canton Road, Kowloon

▼

KAI YIN LO: If you are into the expensive ethnic look, you will love Kai Yin Lo. Her designs are one-of-a-kind accessories—necklaces, earrings, belts, and some gift items. There is little that costs less than $100. Ms. Lo has positioned herself between the serious jewelry market and fun jewelry. Her necklaces and earrings are made with semiprecious stones and gold, thus necessitating a high price. There really is no competition in this style or price range in Hong Kong.

KAI YIN LO

The Peninsula Hotel, Salisbury Road, Kowloon

Mandarin Oriental Hotel, 5 Connaught Road Central, Hong Kong

The Mall at Pacific Place, 88 Queensway, Hong Kong (MTR: Admiralty)

▼

WALTER MA: Young, hip fashions that could be at home in Milan. Prices are moderate. This guy has some great ideas. There's a boutique in Daimaru, Causeway Bay. The Vee line is also designed by Walter Ma, with emphasis on "young." You should have a great figure to wear these outfits.

WALTER MA

16 Wellington Street, Hong Kong

New World Shopping Centre, 18–24 Salisbury Road, Kowloon

▼

BEN YEUNG: A graduate of UCLA, Yeung studied and designed in Europe. In 1981 he established Benny's Fashion and Design Centre Ltd. to sell to the European and Hong Kong markets. Since that time he has established offices in London, Paris, and Milan where the Cigale and Ben Yeung label is being sold.

BEN YEUNG, Hong Kong Designer's Gallery, Paliburg Plaza, 66 Yee Wo Street, Causeway Bay, Hong Kong (MTR: Causeway Bay)

▼

BEN SPROUT: If we were any more cynical, we'd say that Ken Done—the famous Australian graphic artist, advertising maven, and designer—is doing business in Hong Kong as Ben Sprout. There are tiny Ben Sprout boutiques popping up in very obvious tourist neighborhoods, like the Star Ferry terminals and Stanley Market (this is not an outlet store), and these stores sell wonderfully designed, absolutely adorable T-shirts, sweats, and coffee mugs with bold, artistic prints at prices only tourists will pay. Prices are not expensive; they are merely high considering that you can buy less well-designed, but similar, merchandise for much less money.

BEN SPROUT
Star Ferry Terminal, Hong Kong
Star Ferry Terminal, Kowloon
Stanley Market, Stanley Market Road, Hong Kong

▼

GIORDANO: The local unisex version of Benetton, offering jeans, polo shirts, Ts, and sweaters in great colors at very moderate prices. There's a branch every place you look. Even on Granville Road (No. 34)—and this is not a discount outlet. Prices are the same at all shops. The easiest branch to spot is the one below, located on the Golden Mile stretch of Nathan Road.

GIORDANO, 46–52 Nathan Road, Kowloon

Up-and-coming Talent

More and more young designers are finding that Hong Kong is a fine place to be discovered. The local heroes listed above have paved the way, and serve as role models and teachers.

Although many of the young designers below are not yet represented in boutiques, they are busy designing private-label goods for large stores. You may never have heard their names, but we think that is just temporary. You just might be buying the next Christian Lacroix.

You can find the latest and wildest designs by these hot young talents in the shops that line Kimberley Road and Austin Avenue. These two streets, in the northern end of Tsim Sha Tsui, have become the SoHo of Hong Kong. The decor of the shops is avant-garde; the prices are affordable. Start at the corner of Austin and Nathan roads, walking east. Austin Road turns a corner and becomes Austin Avenue, which will turn again and become Kimberley Road heading back toward Nathan Road. We have listed some of our favorite boutiques under "Finds" (see page 193). We also have a tour (see page 260) that names even more.

Another great place to search out talented new designers is a store called **HONG KONG DESIGNER'S GALLERY.** The main shop is in the New Territories, at the Hotel Riverside Plaza Arcade, Tai Chung Kiu Road, Sha Tin. This is quite a bit out of the way for most tourists. A smaller but much more convenient shop is located at Paliburg Plaza, 66 Yee Wo Street (MTR: Causeway Bay). Here you will find bits and pieces from many up-and-coming designer lines. At last visit, Designer's Gallery represented Alan Chu, Judy Mann, Jolie by Ada

Kuen, Jopej by John Cheng, Batik by Candy Solabarrieta, Eldy Pang, and Mayee Lok.

While shopping, watch for labels from designers whose names we predict will be making headway on the international scene before long. Some names to watch for: Laurence Tang, Paul Cheung, Danny Yu, Jennifer Kwok, Bernard Foong, and Shirley Chan.

Finds

S ome of our favorite stores do not fall into any one particular category. Some we love so much that we have to tell you about them again. The following shops are all favorites of ours for one reason or another:

ASHNEIL: A favorite resource for dressy handbags in leather, skin, and sequins for those who want Judith Leiber copycat bags. The shop is amazingly small, but so are the bags. There is a display case with samples of styles; other colors are stored below. Prices range from $150 to $500, although you can negotiate if you are a good customer. Don't mind the fact that this mall is a dump. It's safe and only one block from the Regent.

ASHNEIL, Far East Mansion (1st floor), 5–6 Middle Road, Kowloon

▼

CROCODILE/CROCO-KIDS: Guess what the logo looks like? Crocodile has gone after the Lacoste look in a big way. They have their own big, bright, shiny stores and their own credit cards. With the Crocodile credit card you get a 10% discount on regularly priced items at Crocodile stores, City Sports stores, and the Palm Restaurant. There is a fee of about $7 for the initial card. Children's clothing is fun and colorful. We prefer the men's line to the women's. A polo shirt costs under $20.

CROCODILE/CROCO-KIDS, Hyatt Regency Hong Kong (basement), 67 Nathan Road, Kowloon

▼

JOYCE: Ah, Joyce... our favorite retailer in Hong Kong. Joyce has two of her own boutiques and owns the licenses to big-name designers' shops, including Giorgio Armani, Emporio Armani, Krizia, Genny, Missoni, Sonia Rykiel, Fendi, Maud Frizon, and Issey Miyake. The majority of her shops are in The Landmark, with others in Swire House, The Peninsula, and New World Shopping Centre. Visiting Joyce's shops is a must, especially at sale time.

JOYCE, The Landmark, 16 Des Voeux Road Central, Hong Kong

▼

LEVANTE: Ladies who wear larger sizes will love it here. The shop specializes in washable silks and knits that are flowing and very generously cut. A friend who normally wears a medium and is 5'8" tall took a small. Prices are fair and you can easily put together an outfit for under $100.

LEVANTE, Star House, Canton Road, Kowloon

▼

M GROUP: M Group is actually a chain of stores under the names Birds, Sports Connection, Circles, Cacharel, Children's Clothing

Company, and Attitude. The branch that attracts us the most is Birds. They carry casual, breezy, young fashions. Prices are very moderate as well. Many Birds boutiques will also have a corner devoted to one of the other companies, usually Sports Connection.

M GROUP/BIRDS
The Landmark, 16 Des Voeux Road Central, Hong Kong
Harbour City/Ocean Centre, 5 Canton Road, Kowloon

▼

NAG TRADE LIMITED: The British are renowned for their fine saddles, boots, and riding gear. If you are one of the horsey set, you must come to Nag Trade and feel the goods. The shop is located on the 2nd floor of Star House, and is cluttered with bridles, saddles, boots, britches, and other equestrian trimmings. A mother and her daughter run the shop and are extremely anxious to help. You can have custom riding boots that are butter-soft and durable made for under $200. Riding shirts are also custom-made. The owners are the only agents in Hong Kong for British equestrian supplies, so prices can be kept low. Shipping is no problem. You can also request a catalogue and order from home.

NAG TRADE LIMITED, Star House, Canton Road, Kowloon

▼

LE POMMIER: *Le pommier* in French is the apple tree, and signifies the temptations you will find here. The owner, Prudence Moore, travels to Europe for the designer shows and returns to do her own version of what is in style. There are not many sizes, but if you see something you like and it doesn't fit, usually you can have it made. You have several options in both fabric and design. Many clients are repeaters, and she shops with them in mind. Accessories that are Chanel look-alikes line the walls. We bought a belt that would pass scrutiny (except that it had no CCs) for one third the price of an original. We want to make clear that these are not copies, just similar designs. All accessories come from Europe. Shopping here is like having your own couturier.

LE POMMIER, 39A Wellington Street, Hong Kong

▼

ZHENCHAXUAN/THE BEST TEA HOUSE COMPANY LTD.: Tea is such an important part of Chinese life that it only makes sense that tea utensils are too. We found this very special shop on our Lai Chi Kok outlet day. It is between Splendid and Leighton Stock Sales on Tung Chau West Street. Inside you will find the most wonderful array of teas and Yixing pottery teapots. Some of them are new and some are collector's pieces, signed and documented in a book that the owner keeps to show the artist and his work. The antique and fine-art pots cost $500–$3,000. A small pot is $50–$100. There is another shop in Tsim Sha Tsui, but we prefer the one in Lai Chi Kok.

ZHENCHAXUAN, China Hong Kong City (Tower 1, 8th floor), 33 Canton Road, Kowloon

THE BEST TEA HOUSE COMPANY LTD., 1039–1041 Tung Chau West Street (ground floor), Kowloon (MTR: Lai Chi Kok)

Made-to-Measure for Him

Any gentleman who comes to Hong Kong and doesn't indulge in at least one be-spoke shirt or suit has missed one of the island's pleasures. It is the British way, and the Hong Kong way. It can be an inexpensive or an expensive way, depending upon your personal quality standards.

There are more tailors in Hong Kong than anywhere else in the world. Many of the better tailors learn their trade as they are growing up. It is a family tradition. Others just see a good thing for what it is and jump in. The important thing for you to do is to distinguish between these two types of tailors. Cheap prices usually mean inferior work. But there are exceptions: One of the favored tailors in Hong Kong has so many "under tailors" working for him that he can afford to turn out his garments for a very good price. Smaller tailor shops, where time and energy are spent producing a garment, are more expensive.

Our best advice comes from a friend who lives in Hong Kong. He feels that although many tailors have the ability to construct a good suit, there are only a handful who understand Western tailoring and the Caucasian male or female body. The well-known tailors are well known for a reason: A bargain is not a bargain if it doesn't fit.

▼ Start your search for a tailor the minute you arrive. Leave yourself time for three fittings while in Hong Kong. The first will be for measurements and choice of fabrics; the second fitting will be a loose fabric or muslin fitting; the third will be to detail the finished garment. Shirts sometimes take only two fittings, and then you receive the finished goods after arriving home. When ordering a suit, keep in mind your lifestyle at home and when you plan to wear it.

▼ Most tailors carry a full line of imported fabrics from Italy, England, and France. Ask whether the thread they use is imported also. If it is not, ask to see the quality, and test it for durability. Remember all those horror stories you have heard about suits falling apart? It wasn't the fabric; it was the thread.

▼ Check the quality of the lining. The better tailors have beautiful choices in lining fabrics, some imported and some not, but all in good taste. Be sure to specify a fully lined jacket.

▼ Check the inner-lining material to make sure it is stiff enough to hold the shape of the suit.

▼ Check the quality of the shoulder pads, the buttons, and the buttonholes. A tailor could save a lot of money by using inferior goods. A bad tailor cannot make a good buttonhole.

▼ Well-made suits from a Hong Kong tailor are no longer as inexpensive as they used to be. Imported fabrics run about $20–$80 per yard, and an average-sized suit will take 3½ yards. The silk/wool blends and cashmeres cost more. The finished price for a suit will run in the area of $200–$800. You could do better in some cases with an off-the-rack suit in the United States, but the quality would not be the same. Ask for tailoring prices with and without the material. In some cases you might wish to supply your own. At the very least, you will know what the tailor is charging for labor versus cost.

▼ The shop will want a 50% deposit to start the work. If less is demanded, the suit will probably be turned out by a manufacturing house. Finished shirts will run $25–$75 depending upon your choice of material and style. French cuffs cost more than plain ones. White collars cost extra.

▼ If you are having the tailor ship the suits to you, remember to figure in the Customs charges and shipping. On average, it costs $20 per suit to air-freight them to you. Shirts can be shipped for $30 per dozen. Once you have established an account with a tailor or a shirtmaker and he has your measurements on file, you can simply get the fabric swatches sent to you for the new season and do your shopping through the mail—or in a local hotel.

▼ Check to see if the tailor you have chosen makes trips to the United States to visit customers. Chances are, if you live in a major city (New York, Washington, Los Angeles, or Chicago), he will. Most of the tailors we recommend either come in person once a year or send a representative with fabric books and order forms. At that time, new measurements can be taken in case you have lost or gained weight. However, we recommend making only minor changes. Any major change should be done in Hong Kong, where a new muslin can be cut.

▼ The tailors we recommend have been tried and tested by one of us, our husbands, relatives, or friends. There are many other tailors in Hong Kong. There is at least one in every hotel shopping arcade. There are even tailors who set up booths at the various night markets. Unless you have a personal recommendation, we say "Beware." Your suit might be cheap, but will it be good?

The Big Three

H. BAROMON LTD.: Tycoon alert: This is a No. 8 warning. If you wonder where the real financial heavyweights have their clothing made, wonder no more. H. Baromon has been in the business for forty years, serving the elite. His reputation is so above the rest of the world that we are surprised his shop hasn't been moved to Savile Row. When you go to choose suit fabric from H. Baromon, you receive a little booklet containing a photo of the shop, a brief description of the H. Baromon philosophy, a page where you can paste your sample cutting, a memo page for notes, a dollar conversion chart, and a very nice map to help you find your way back.

A made-to-order suit takes at least seven days. The average suit price is over $750. Shirts average $100. H. Baromon does not send representatives to the United States.

H. BAROMON LTD., Swire House, Connaught Road Central, Hong Kong

▼

A-MAN HING CHEONG CO. LTD.: Fondly referred to as "Ah-men," this tailor shop in the Mandarin Oriental Hotel turns out quite a few garments for the rich-tourist-and-businessman trade, and therefore has become very adept at relating to the European-cut suit. They don't even blink twice when you ask for an extra pair of trousers. They just smile and ask for more money. The prices here are on the higher side, with a suit costing about $650. However, the quality is excellent, and that is what you are paying for. Anyone can buy off the rack. This is a Savile Row–quality suit.

A-Man will also do custom shirts for approximately $50. If you wish to cable them, their cable name is "Luckylucky." You will feel lucky lucky when you get home and enjoy your new bespoke clothing.

A-MAN HING CHEONG CO. LTD., Mandarin Oriental Hotel, 5 Connaught Road Central, Hong Kong

W. W. CHAN & SONS TAILOR LTD.:
Our personal choice (and our husbands'), is
W. W. Chan. Peter Chan carries on a family
business, which he has built and expanded
with a recent acquisition. Although the main
shop and the women's tailoring offices are on
Nathan Road, across the street from the mosque,
Chan has bought George Chen's tailor business
in The Peninsula Hotel and converted Chen
from an upscale tailor to one of the Big Three.
Thereby making it the Big Four. Men who
require a luxury address and surroundings will
appreciate George Chen's showroom. Prices
and quality are equal to what you get at W. W.
Chan. The average price for a suit is about $500.

What you also get at W. W. Chan is adventure. Just a walk up the staircase is an adventure. (The elevator is in the back, on the first
floor of the arcade, near the Opal Mine.) Chan's
Kowloon showroom can best be described as
casual. Which makes it all the more
fun.... Finding one of the Big Three in re-
laxed surroundings guarantees that the price
you pay for the suit goes into the suit, not the
overhead. Not that the place is shabby (it isn't),
it's just that the Chan family has its eye on
fabric, service, and quality . . . not wallpaper.
There are zillions of fabrics stacked into the
walls, library style; the atmosphere is not nearly
as uptight as at some other showrooms.

The quality of the Chan product is equal to
its first-rate reputation; customers here tend to
be those who demand the best and like to find
it for themselves. The Bijan crowd may prefer
H. Baromon; the British tycoons may be happier in Central. We aren't happier anywhere
else. We've actually made friends with other
Americans who were having fittings; there is a
constant flow of airline pilots and businessmen
coming through the door. Everyone who comes
here seems to be a member of Peter's fan club.
Single women may want to hang out just to
meet men.

Prices here are exactly the same as at the

other members of the Big Three; gentlemen should expect to pay about $500 total (labor plus fabric) for a two-piece suit. Chan is the only one of the Big Three to have a women's tailor; see Irene's Fashions, page 209. Peter comes to New York twice a year; Eric from George Chen comes once a year. To get on the mailing list for the U.S. schedule, write ahead or fax 011-852-368-2194.

W. W. CHAN & SONS TAILOR LTD., Burlington House (2nd floor), 94 Nathan Road, Kowloon

Made-to-Measure: Shirts

ASCOT CHANG CO. LTD.: This well-known shirtmaker has many branches in Hong Kong and Kowloon. The shops are filled with wonderful fabrics imported from Switzerland and France. Prices are competitive with David's; they offer mail-order once your measurements have been taken. Shirts run between $40 and $125 depending upon the fabric and style. Top of the line.

ASCOT CHANG CO. LTD.
The Peninsula Hotel, Salisbury Road, Kowloon
The Regent Hotel, Salisbury Road, Kowloon
Prince's Building, Chater Road, Hong Kong

▼

DAVID'S SHIRTS: David's is one of the most popular and famous custom shirt shops in Hong Kong. (They also have a branch in New York City.) The main shop in Hong Kong is in Kowloon, on Kimberley Road. We don't think it is the most convenient, however, and usually shop in the Mandarin Oriental Hotel branch. That shop is tiny and crowded with fabrics standing side by side, like soldiers in a British regiment. The fabric colors are muted, and may at first glance seem rather ordinary. As each bolt is brought out and unraveled, however, the quality of the fabrics and subtleties of design become apparent. If you didn't know better you would swear you were in London.

For custom shirts, two fittings are necessary—one for the measurements and then one with the garment. David's will copy any favorite shirt you may have. Just bring it with you and plan to leave it. They also have a framed illustration of collar and cuff styles you can choose from. Mail-order is not only possible but common with repeat customers. If you cannot get to Hong Kong, ask for a current swatch and price list. Return a shirt that fits you perfectly and a check, along with fabric and collar/cuff choices. Approximately four to six weeks later a box of new shirts will arrive. If you want to contact their New York store call (212) 757-1803.

DAVID'S SHIRTS
  Mandarin Oriental Hotel, 5 Connaught Road Central, Hong Kong
  Wing Lee Building (ground floor), 33 Kimberley Road, Kowloon

More Tailors

GEORGE CHEN: George Chen's shop is on the mezzanine in The Peninsula Hotel, and is very nice indeed. It also comes with a secret. About a year ago, Mr. Chen retired and sold this business to Peter Chan, who uses his W. W. Chan workshops to make the George Chen clothes. Which means that this is technically one of the Big Three. Prices are the same as at W. W. Chan, but the ambience is dressier.

Women, please note: Danny Chen (whom we swear by) is at the W. W. Chan address only, and is not the women's tailor for George Chen. Nor is he related.

GEORGE CHEN, The Peninsula Hotel, Salisbury Road, Kowloon

▼

JIMMY CHEN: Not to be confused with George or Danny, Jimmy Chen has a good reputation and nice shops in the city's best tourist locations. His shop is especially known for making a little of everything: suits, shirts, men's clothes, and women's clothes. He also makes cotton summer suits for men, which many other tailors refuse to do. Prices are equal to those charged by the Big Three.

JIMMY CHEN
> The Landmark, Edinburgh Tower, 16 Des Voeux Road Central, Hong Kong
> The Peninsula Hotel, Salisbury Road, Kowloon
> Harbour City/Omni The Hong Kong Hotel, Kowloon

▼

GIEVES & HAWKES: This is our fave: ever heard of bringing coals to Newcastle? Here you have one of the most famous Savile Row tailors opening shop in Hong Kong, the city where tailors commit their lives to bettering Savile Row. Gieves & Hawkes does a very good business with those who do not trust a Chinese tailor (silly chaps) and who want the status associated with one of London's veddy, veddy best.

GIEVES & HAWKES
> Prince's Building, Chater Road, Hong Kong
> The Peninsula Hotel, Salisbury Road, Kowloon

SAM'S TAILOR: Sam is the most famous tailor in Hong Kong, and he has no qualms about letting you know that. Sam is, in fact, three people, a father and two sons, all Sam. We have met all three on various visits, and they are all quite charming. Sam's is well known for good prices (suits average $200–$300) and service. They have a large staff cutting and sewing in their workroom. A suit can usually be finished in three days. If the showroom in the Burlington Arcade is not overflowing with customers, you can chat about fabrics, styles, and prices with one of the owners. Most people who come in order a suit or shirts or both. Don't forget to look at the photographs of Sam's famous clientele; they boast of princes and dignitaries from all over the world. Sam's is fun. If you are coming to Hong Kong on a cruise ship, you will probably meet Sam. He or a group of his staff fly to the port of origin, take orders, do fittings, and then return to make the garments. By the time the ship arrives in Hong Kong, everyone has a suit or two—or three—waiting for them. Pretty good business.

SAM'S TAILOR, Burlington Arcade, 92–94 Nathan Road, Kowloon

▼

YING TAI LTD.: Coming to Ying Tai is like coming to a party where you are the guest of honor. The shop in the Hilton Hotel is enormous, has big showroom windows opening on to the 1st floor arcade, and is full of tailors and sales staff so that you don't ever have to wait. Like the shop, the selection of fabrics for suits and shirts is enormous. The work done is excellent, and the staff is used to working with the Western figure. There is another shop in The Peninsula Hotel. Suit prices start at $300.

YING TAI LTD., Hong Kong Hilton Hotel, 2 Queen's Road Central, Hong Kong

Made-to-Measure for Her

Men have been having suits made in Hong Kong for years, but women are still learning the ropes. Finding a tailor who can properly drape fabric on a womanly Western figure takes a lot of doing.

We began with **W. W. CHAN** for the simple reason that Peter Chan makes our husbands' clothes. But there is method to our madness; we didn't just pick an agreeable face from our circle of friends. The three best men's tailors in Hong Kong (see page 199) are so defined because they have their own workshops; only Chan makes women's clothing.

There are scads of tailors in town who will take on curvy clients; possibly some of them can tailor a suit to your liking. You can find tailors less expensive than the Big Three. But for women who want the best, only W. W. Chan will make you a suit that fits like couture.

When you pick a tailor in Hong Kong, know the rules of the game: Absolutely every hand-made garment in Hong Kong with the exception of those from the Big Three is contracted out as piecework. In piecework, seamstresses and tailors are paid by the piece, not by the hour. It behooves them to finish quickly. They do not have time to press individual seams; to move slowly; to do painstaking work.

The Big Three pay their tailors by the hour, and will accept only the best, because their clients insist on it. Work is not farmed out but made on the premises. A French atelier or Savile Row would not be any more professional. The quality of the garments from these workrooms is superior on every garment cut.

Men's and women's clothing costs differ at W. W. Chan. You are charged a flat rate for the making of the garment (no matter what size or how complicated); you pay for the fabric by the yard (or provide your own). A woman's suit totals about $350. A dress costs about $170 for labor alone, a jacket, $175.

While three fittings are recommended, especially for a first-timer, the truth is that these guys can get it more or less perfect after the first measurements are taken.

"Usually fit perfectly," says Danny.

We would have had some women's clothing made at other tailors, but the truth is, we were frightened off. The two other tailors we took seriously did not pass muster after we inspected recently finished garments on their new owners.

▼ If you know you want to use Danny Chen, it's best to write, call, or fax ahead for an appointment. If you aren't headed for Hong Kong, ask about being fitted in the U.S., since Mr. Chen travels to major cities once a year. Men can book with Peter Chan. Contact W. W. Chan & Sons Tailor Ltd., A-2, 2/F, Burlington House, 94 Nathan Road, Kowloon, Hong Kong. From the U.S. phone 011-852-366-9738 or fax 011-852-368-2194; cable WWCHAN. You can always drop in, of course, but if your time is limited or you need to work at odd hours, an appointment is smart.

▼ If your mind is not made up as to what tailor you want to use, spend your first day in Hong Kong visiting shops, looking at the samples, asking questions, and feeling goods. Because you should schedule three fittings, you'll need at least three days to have a garment made; five days is preferable. Try to see clothes being fitted on other people, which isn't as hard as it sounds. You don't have to climb into the dressing room, but watch the public part to see the fit between garment and owner. A well-made garment is worthless if it doesn't flatter the wearer.

▼ Tailors make tailored clothing best. Don't ask them to make a knit bodysuit or a Diane

Freis–style dress with flounces and crystal pleating. Danny Chen will make a bodysuit with finished facing (you must provide the knit; there is none in Hong Kong) at the same charge as a blouse ($75 for labor), but he prefers not to.

▼ All tailors sell fabric by the yard; the better the tailor, the better the quality and selection of his goods. Be advised that tailors are geared for men's suits and not women's clothing, so fabric choices for ladies can be limited.

▼ If you bring fabric with you, make sure you have enough. (See our chart on page 209.) If you bring a fabric with nap, a large pattern, or a plaid, or if you are larger than size 14, bring more yardage. If you are buying fabric in Hong Kong, it is easiest if you buy from your tailor, but by no means essential. Allow more time so you don't feel pressured.

▼ Bring your own buttons and trim if you want top-of-the-line polish to your suit. Every tailor in town can make a Chanel-style suit, but none look as classy as the real thing, for lack of proper buttons and trims.

▼ Have all measurements taken so that you may reorder or have additional items made at a later date without a return trip to Hong Kong. Mail delivery from Hong Kong happens to be safe and efficient. Most tailors use air freight, which costs you about $50.

▼ If you care enough to use a master like Danny Chen, have enough sense to listen to what he has to say. He'll make whatever you insist that he make, but if you're smart you'll listen to him before you make a costly mistake. "Suits that look bad have only two problems," he says. "Wrong fabric or wrong style for body."

FABRICATIONS

FABRIC WIDTH	GARMENT	YARDAGE
44″	long-sleeved dress	4½ yards
44″	blouse	2½ to 3 yards
54″–60″	trousers/woolen	1½ yards
54″–60″	blazer	2 yards
54″–60″	pleated skirt with jacket	3 to 4½ yards
60″ knit	long-sleeved bodysuit	2 yards

Women's Tailors

IRENE'S FASHIONS: In Hong Kong, a city where locals often think Americans are inscrutable, you'll find some unusual marketing practices. Thus it is that W. W. Chan, known as a men's tailor, has a women's division in the same shop, but this tailor has a secondary name (Irene's Fashions) so that customers will know there is a women's tailor on hand. Clothes made at Irene's are made on the premises, which means this is the only one of the Big Three to make women's clothing. Don't mind if some of the women's samples hanging around are a bit dowdy; for the lowdown on having something made here, see page 206.

IRENE'S FASHIONS, Burlington Arcade (2nd floor), 92–94 Nathan Road, Kowloon

▼

MODE ELEGANTE: Of all of the zillions of tailors we went to in search of women's clothing, this was the only one who had samples that were not only stunning but were true fashion, not pale imitations. While we did not have anything made (we use Danny Chen exclusively), we were impressed. We know clients who swear by this source.

MODE ELEGANTE, The Peninsula Hotel, Salisbury Road, Kowloon

▼

PRINCE'S TAILOR: Our friend Isabelle decided on Prince's because her friend living in Hong Kong brought her here. She was pleased with the work, although one of the skirts she ordered was not in the length she asked for, and she refused to pay for it. (No problem.) The suit she had made was copied from a suit she brought with her, in the tailor's fabric, and consisted of a large blazer with a tiny miniskirt. Since Isabelle is a size 2, she hardly tied up a lot of money in yard goods, and her entire bill for the one finished suit was about $250. When we inspected the suit, we pronounced it fine but not thrilling. It was better than fine, but it in no way compared with the quality of the W. W. Chan suit we had made.

PRINCE'S TAILOR, Sheraton Hotel Shopping Arcade, Salisbury Road, Kowloon

▼

SAM'S TAILOR: We went to the famous Sam's for a women's blazer, and quite possibly would have had one made, since Sam's reputation for quality work at a low price is excellent. The truth is, while we were standing in this incredibly tiny shop, another Western woman was being fitted in her new navy suit, and did not like how it looked on her. When it came down to it, we were not able to part with our hard-earned money.

When we asked about a navy gabardine blazer, we were told that such a blazer had just been made for Elizabeth Taylor and could be ours in forty-eight hours for about $150. When we said we had to think about it, we were very pleasantly reminded that Joan Collins also had such a blazer from Sam.

SAM'S TAILOR, Burlington Arcade, 92–94 Nathan Road, Kowloon

Made-to-Measure: Shoes and Leathergoods

I f you are a shoe fanatic, read carefully, because there's no business like shoe business in Hong Kong.

First things first: In Hong Kong, shoes are usually sized in the European manner. There are few, if any, women's shoes above a size 40 (U.S. 9½). American and European women with large feet spend a lot of their time in Hong Kong complaining about the difficulties in finding shoes. If you wear a large size, and are in an emergency situation, the good news is that the Marks & Spencer department stores carry large-sized shoes (up to size 10 or 10½). These are private-label, not designer, styles but they are good, "sensible" English shoes, and are reasonably priced at around $50 a pair.

We remain disappointed in the shoes available on Leighton Road in Happy Valley. Locals keep recommending this area, but to us these shoes, with their "Made in Italy" labels, are one more of Hong Kong's scams. The shoes are manufactured in Hong Kong and then printed with Italian labels. Expect that they will not last that long. However, at these prices you might not care how long they last. For the most part, these are inexpensive copies of fashion styles. They sell for about $40–$60 a pair. We vote a "pass" on Leighton Road.

There are many European shoe boutiques in Hong Kong, and many of them have quality goods at prices about 20% lower than in the

United States. Charles Jourdan has an extensive stock at savings against U.S. prices. Gucci we find more expensive; Bally is about similar. Finely crafted leathergoods are equally available at the designer boutiques. They just aren't at bargain prices.

You may find shoes and handbags in Stanley Market; many more handbags are sold in the Lanes.

We investigated having shoes made and came up with both satisfied and not-so-satisfied customers. The latest rumors are that the made-to-measure shoe business is dying in Hong Kong because the last makers have all gone to Japan, where they make more money.

Custom shoe shops usually look like holes in the wall, junked up with dusty shoes. Even the fanciest ones in the fanciest hotels don't look like John Lobb in London. If you really want shoes made, ignore the surroundings and walk in. The shoes you see displayed are samples of what can be made. Some people come to Hong Kong with shoes and ask to have them copied. Others decide once they are there, and have no idea what they want. All of the custom shops have similar policies:

▼Once you have decided on a style, a canvas will be made of your foot. This will then be turned into a mold from which the shoe will be made. If the shoemaker you have chosen simply takes measurements, leave. This is not what you are paying for. You won't be happy with the results.

▼ Unless you specifically ask to pick out your skins the shoemaker will do it for you. We suggest you pick your own and mark the backs so that no one else will use them. In the case of leather, ask to see the hides and examine the quality. Be able to verify that your skins were indeed used.

▼ Many kinds of leather or skin are used in making exotic shoes and boots. The following cannot legally be shipped into the United States: kangaroo, elephant, shark, antelope, gnu, sea lion, lizard, sea turtle, or alligator.

▼ The shoemaker usually has a base price list from which he works. A basic pair of men's cordovans cost $150, say. Then you add the extras. This is especially true of boots, where you might decide to have fur lining ($20), zipper sides ($5), or double leather soles ($4). If a man's foot is bigger than 12½, a special quote will be made.

▼ If you are having shoes shipped to you, allow for shipping charges. Surface mail postage for shoes or a handbag should cost $15. Airmail for the same will be $20–$30.

▼ The shoemaker will want a deposit (at least one third, possibly one half) or full payment before he starts to make the shoes. This is negotiable depending upon the store.

▼ If at all possible, pick up your shoes yourself. If they are uncomfortable, it is easier to remedy the problem while you are there.

▼ Prices vary from $20 to $100 from shop to shop. Some shops will bargain; others will not.

▼ Made-to-measure shoes are usually more expensive than U.S. designer or top-of-the-line brand shoes.

We tried to have shoes and a handbag made in Hong Kong, but after visiting several shops and working with several reputable makers, we simply gave up. With size 10½B feet—maybe even size 11 (all that walking can make them swell)—and with perfect fit and everlasting happiness with our Ferragamos and Reeboks, we were reluctant to plunk down $200 for a pair of simple low-heeled calf shoes. The same shoes from Ferragamo cost about $150. Who needs the extra aggravation on a short trip?

The case of the handbag was even more interesting, because we had with us a real

Chanel bag, and wanted it copied, line for line. Our model did not come with Cs embroidered on it in the first place, so we weren't talking copyright violation or anything shady. We just wanted the same size and style. Not one of the five places we went to could come up with quality hardware that would make the bag look as expensive as the real thing. They had the leather; they could quilt. They didn't have hardware (without Cs) that could pass muster; the chains were cheap-looking and far too yellow.

For the record, Hermès Kelly bags look great at many sources.

There are, however, several places we do stop in at whenever we're looking for a particular style shoe or bag:

SAM WO, Li Yuen Street West, Hong Kong: We take no credit for having found this delicious man; to us, this will always be Rose's place. Rose has been buying here for years; Sam asks more than some of the other stand dealers, but Rose has learned that the quality of Sam's bags is higher. We bought a bag similar to hers from another stand, and were shocked at how much better hers was. Thank you, Rose; thanks, Sam.

KWONG WING CO., 21 Li Yuen Street East, Hong Kong: This is a store behind the stalls that sells pretty much the going thing. Quality is not so high as at Sam's, but prices can be 50% lower. Inspect carefully; note that some of the chains on Chanel bags can be rather yellow and cheap-looking. The Epi-style Vuitton (colored pieces) comes in a zillion styles and a wide enough price range to allow you to stock up on gifts. However, discriminating shoppers can tell this is not real Vuitton.

LEE'S, Stalls No. 58 & 59, Li Yuen Street East, Hong Kong: This stall at the top of Li Yuen Street East sells a great Chanel-style bag for about $15. Honest.

MAYER SHOE COMPANY, Mandarin Oriental Hotel, 5 Connaught Road Central, Hong Kong: European-styled shoes and handbags sold in such a pleasant atmosphere, without hype, that it is a delight to shop here. They understand the Ralph Lauren school of elegance perfectly. They have shoes in stock or will make a pair for you. Our choice.

LILY SHOES, The Peninsula Hotel, Salisbury Road, Kowloon; and Kowloon Hotel Shopping Arcade, 19–21 Nathan Road, Kowloon: Lily has a huge reputation among Westerners, probably because one of their shops is in the ever-convenient Peninsula Hotel. Prices are high for Hong Kong, but moderate when compared to the rest of the world. (A Chanel-style handbag: $175 from Lily; $795 from Chanel.) They will make women's shoes for about $200 a pair. The store in the Kowloon Hotel Shopping Arcade is always empty and will bargain with you; the one in the Peninsula is mobbed and not too big on customer service. Frankly, they leave us cold.

LEE KEE SHOES AND BOOTS, 65 Peking Road, Kowloon: Another big name, especially for men's shoes. We have seen nice shoes from this source, but our last visit did not leave us with an enthusiastic feeling.

SHOEMAN LAU, Hyatt Regency Hotel Shopping Arcade, 67 Nathan Road, Kowloon: The best bet for men's made-to-measure shoes, with an international reputation to match.

VIP SHOES, The Regent Hotel Shopping Arcade, Salisbury Road, Kowloon: Uncle Lennie adores his shoes from here and can't wait to go back for more.

DANELLI & PITTI, Kowloon Hotel Shopping Arcade, 19–21 Nathan Road, Kowloon: This handbag store has such refreshing merchandise that we just had to include it—a silk Kelly bag for $200 that's drop-dead chic is too creative to ignore.

TORINO, The Regent Hotel Shopping Arcade, Salisbury Road, Kowloon: The most incredible skin bags we have ever seen anywhere in the world are sold in this shop, at prices that may make you shudder. Although the store claims that alligator and crocodile are the same thing (of course they're not), they do provide permits so you can import your bag to the States. We are talking several thousand dollars for such a bag, but that is the going price. The colors are unbelievable. The sales help is not very friendly, but the store is a find if you live and die by expensive bags.

Continental Big-Name Leathergoods (not easily found in the U.S.)

COMTESSE: Leathergoods handmade in Germany and considered a major status symbol by both Europeans and Japanese. If you believe in a very expensive bag that makes a statement, and your goal is to have something different from everyone else's, this store is a must. The line is also sold at Duty Free Shoppers.

COMTESSE
   The Landmark, 16 Des Voeux Road Central, Hong Kong
   The Peninsula Hotel, Salisbury Road, Kowloon

▼

LANCEL: A big name in France for well-made handbags and leathergoods that often have the heavy stitching of the chic country look. Their group with white stitching on dark leather is timeless. Sold in several Japanese

department stores because of the appeal to
that market, but also in their own shops, which
are either in hotel arcades or in the giant
Ocean Cities mall.

LANCEL, Harbour City/Ocean Terminal, Canton Road, Kowloon

▼

LONGCHAMP: French leathergoods that
aren't overdone in the U.S. but are a huge
status symbol in parts of the Orient. Their
refined sporty elegance gets a lot of attention.
The rich man's Dooney & Bourke.

LONGCHAMP
The Regent Hotel, Salisbury Road, Kowloon
The Peninsula Hotel, Salisbury Road, Kowloon

▼

LOEWE: They are standing three deep at the
counters, and they are not American.

LOEWE, The Peninsula Hotel, Salisbury Road,
Kowloon

Jewelry and Gemstones

H ong Kong trades every variety and quality of gemstone. It is the fifth-largest
diamond-cutting center in the world. The
money changing hands in this industry
totals billions of dollars per year.

The good news about buying gemstones in
Hong Kong is that you can bring them (unset)
back to the United States for a negligible duty
(or for no duty at all). The bad news is that
finding good stones requires a Ph.D. in gemol-

ogy. You'll also require Sherlock Holmes at your side, and a jeweler's loupe. Actually, what you need is someone like our friend Elizabeth Li, who has family in the business and explained it all to us.

The jewelry and gemstone businesses are separate, and converge only at the wholesale level, where you will never be admitted without a bona fide dealer. If you are serious about buying stones, you should be introduced to the wholesale dealers. This requires personal contact from a dealer here, or from a friend who is Chinese and living in Hong Kong. It is a very tight business. Don't expect to just walk into a shop off the street and see the best stones or get the best prices.

We have many jewelers we actually trust in Hong Kong. However, our trust has been earned through experience. Friends who live there have their favorite people and have been kind enough to share sources with us. Other friends have been buying from one family or firm for fifty years and have shared sources with us. There is risk in every purchase; but if you are dealing with a reputable jeweler that risk is minimized. Reputation is everything. If you are looking for good pearls, diamonds, opals, jade, or ivory, educate yourself first. Take the time to learn before you leap.

Jewelry

Jewelry is the word we use to describe decorative baubles made of gold and either precious or semiprecious stones. There are almost as many jewelry shops in Hong Kong as there are tailors. As you walk down almost any street in Hong Kong, your eyes are constantly drawn to windows full of magnificent pins, rings, and earrings. Much of the Hong Kong jewelry is made with 18K gold, which is popular in Asia. This is a yellower gold than the 14K gold Americans usually prefer. Jewelers used to dealing with overseas clients keep pieces on hand for both markets. Decide which you prefer before you begin serious negotiations on a piece. 14K is less expensive than 18K. Gold will be marked with either a K label or, in the alternative, "375" (9K), "585" (14K), or "750" (18K).

One of the best buys in the jewelry field is in custom-made pieces. If you have a favorite Tiffany, Harry Winston, or Van Cleef & Arpels catalogue, take it with you. A good jeweler can translate any basic design into something just for you—at half the cost. To make certain that you get value for your money we suggest the following:

▼ Look at many things in the shop, both expensive and inexpensive. We discovered a tremendous buy on lapis beads by just being curious. You never know what the jeweler will use as a promotion piece in order to get you going as a client. These beads were selling in Lane Crawford for $250, and we bought them for $60.

▼ Ask questions. If the jeweler is not willing to spend time with you, leave.

▼ Negotiate prices on a few items before you get down to business on the one that you really want. If the jeweler knows that you are looking for a good price at the beginning, the process will happen faster.

▼ Ask if you can get an outside appraisal of the piece of jewelry that you are considering. If the jeweler hesitates, question why.

▼ Remember that you will pay duty on set versus unset stones coming into the United States. Use this as a negotiating tool.

▼ Always get a written certification of the gold content of your piece of jewelry. This is important for insurance and Customs.

▼ Also get a receipt from the store, quoting the exact price that you paid. Don't leave it up to U.S. Customs to evaluate your goods.

▼ If you choose to have the jewelry sent to you, confirm that it will be insured, and for how much.

▼ If you are buying a piece of jewelry with large stones, have a separate appraisal done on them. It should include a photograph and a detailed description of each stone.

The jewelers we recommend are of the larger variety, and reputable. We like them all for different reasons. Many of them carry jade, pearls, and other collector's pieces along with fine jewelry. We have not bought personally from each and every one, but each and every one has been strongly recommended by someone who has. Interview a few of them before settling on one.

Expensive Jewelry

GEMSLAND, Mandarin Oriental Hotel, 5 Connaught Road Central, Hong Kong. A great source for custom work, pearls, and set pieces at fair prices. Ask for Richard Chen or his mother, Mrs. Helen Chen. There is another branch in the Hilton Hotel.

CHARISMA, 1509 Melbourne Plaza, 33 Queen's Road Central, Hong Kong. Good for large custom pieces and unset stones. Derrick Mace is a wholesaler full-time, and has his showroom for custom work within the office. Only serious buyers should go here.

HENRY JEWELLERY LTD., 29 Nathan Road, Kowloon. Where the Beverly Hills ladies like to shop. Set pieces are very elegantly glitzy.

KEVIN, Holiday Inn Golden Mile, 50 Nathan Road, Kowloon, has some very unusual and creative pieces of jewelry. Not the usual stuff you see in the hotel arcade shops.

LARRY JEWELRY, The Landmark, 16 Des Voeux Road Central, Hong Kong. Specializes in glitzy and large pieces. This is a very popular place with the ladies who lunch.

KAI YIN LO, Mandarin Oriental Hotel (mezzanine), 5 Connaught Road Central, Hong Kong. We consider this jewelry with an ethnic flavor to be both serious and fun. Her designs using gold and semiprecious gemstones are unique in Hong Kong. Several branch stores.

Not-so-expensive Jewelry

PAN AM PEARLS: Another of Rose's finds and now in new digs upstairs with a souvenir shop. The *faux* pearls we bought from them are nifty. We got the two-strand matinee length, which we have wanted for some time and have priced in the U.S. at about $200. Here, in beautiful downtown Kowloon: a mere $40. Baroque pearls are also available. This is right near the Hyatt Regency Hong Kong, so don't let the address throw you.

PAN AM PEARLS, 9 Lock Road, Kowloon

▼

JASPER: French jewelry of the artsy kind; expensive as all get-out, but really chic. A small mall shop with very unusual (for Hong Kong) merchandise.

JASPER, The Mall at Pacific Place, 88 Queensway, Hong Kong (MTR: Admiralty)

▼

MADE IN HONG KONG: Made in Hong Kong has a huge showroom in Hung Hom, the factory-outlet district, and is part of many a shopping tour's tour. To say this store specializes in "not-so-expensive jewelry" may be misleading, because the few things we priced were more expensive than our fancy jeweler Richard Chen at Gemsland. You go on a tour of the factory and are then set free in the showroom, where little bargaining is done over the wide selection of OK but boring choices. There's little bargaining, but this is a great place to go to learn more and to establish baseline prices.

MADE IN HONG KONG, Kaiser Estates Phase II, 51 Man Yue Street, Hung Hom

▼

AXESSORIUM: With several shops around town, this tiny chain can give you the Chanel look in affordable variations. We found a necklace of pearls as big as golf balls—the kind that we have only seen in French *Vogue*—for $60: not cheap, but a fair price. Earrings begin around $25, but go to $50 rather rapidly. There are also belts and hair accessories.

AXESSORIUM
Harbour City/Ocean Terminal, Canton Road, Kowloon
Prince's Building, Chater Road, Hong Kong
Houston Centre, 63 Mody Road, Kowloon

Made-to-Measure Jewelry

With a treasure trove of unset gems just growing old in the underwear drawer, we decided to take some gemstones (bought in Brazil) to Hong

Kong and have them made into jewelry. The results were incredible.

We chose Gemsland partly because of the recommendation of a friend, but also because we liked the fact that they weren't tippy top of the line soooo fancy you would be intimidated, or so low and funky that you were frightened.

We walked into the shop in the Mandarin Oriental Hotel without an appointment. Out came the gemstones and the opinions as to what should be done. We had a suite of three green tourmalines, two matched ovals, and one larger stone, emerald cut. We wanted them in one ring, although there was much discussion as to whether or not that was wise. Some were for making them into earrings plus a ring; earrings plus a choker; a ring on prongs; a ring with diamonds; etc.

Finally we were given some clay and started playing with the stones in the clay, molding a ring. A price was quoted ($350), we nervously nodded a go-ahead, and we left.

The next three days were not easy. What if it was ugly? What if we didn't like it? Finally, the big moment. We arrive. We sit. A small silk pouch comes out. Then the ring is revealed.

It is far more gorgeous than ever anticipated!

It also looks far different from what we think we designed.

Who cares?

For $350, this is the best bargain in Hong Kong.

We pay with American Express plastic so as to gain ninety days' free insurance on the Purchase Protection Plan.

Yahoo!

Pearls

If you are searching for pearls and pearls alone, you will have many options. Every jewelry store has them in the window. The question is, Who do you trust? When we were doing our research for *Born to Shop: Tokyo*, we were told that all the pearls that make it to Hong Kong are the rejects from Tokyo. It is true that pearl prices in Tokyo are higher than in Hong Kong, but we don't believe that all the pearls are inferior. The story does, however, point out that some jewelers might be selling inferior quality. Also, whiter pearls are more prized in Hong Kong than pinker or yellower pearls, and are therefore the most expensive.

The bigger jewelry shops are a safe bet for buying quality pearls. The price tag will be higher than on the street, but you have some assurance that, should you have a problem with your second appraisal back home, they will make amends. The following are all considered reputable shops for pearls:

TRIO PEARL, The Peninsula Hotel, Salisbury Road, Kowloon. One of the best places to go to in Hong Kong is Trio, whose reputation for high prices and higher quality is well known.

GEMSLAND, Mandarin Oriental Hotel, 5 Connaught Road Central, Hong Kong. Richard Chen or his mother, Helen, are happy to spend hours rolling pearls to find the best ones. We even know people who mail-ordered pearls and were happy with the quality.

K. S. SZE & SONS, Mandarin Oriental Hotel, 5 Connaught Road Central, Hong Kong. This showroom is so swank it might make you nervous to enter, although it looks fancier from the windows than it does inside. It is a few doors down from Gemsland. While they also sell diamonds and gemstones, they are well known for the quality of their pearls and the fairness of their prices.

Opals

We have only one suggestion when it comes to buying opals: Buyer beware. Opals are mined in Australia, among other places, and brought to Hong Kong to be cut, polished, and shipped out again. Considering this, it is surprising that there are not more opal stores. You will see opals in fine jewelry stores, but you will not see many. One company in particular, **OPAL CREATIONS,** has cornered the tourist opal trade. They have set up one shop in Burlington Arcade, Tsim Sha Tsui, that is a re-creation of an opal mine, with illustrations and samples of what to look for and what not to look for. It is informative and fun, especially if you are with children. The mine opens up into the (surprise!) retail store with opal choices galore. There are big stones and little stones, set stones and unset stones. All the opals are guaranteed to be authentic and not tampered with in any way. Prices are high, and the sales pitch is strong, but for small pieces, there are many choices. Comparison-shop elsewhere before coming, and then bargain once you are there. Opal Creations is on the ground floor of the Burlington Arcade, 92–94 Nathan Road, Tsim Sha Tsui, Kowloon. Otherwise, simply shop in good jewelry stores. It is easy to be duped with opals.

Diamonds

Diamonds come into Hong Kong duty-free from around the world. It is one of the world's largest diamond-trading areas. If you wish to buy diamonds, check with the Hong Kong Tourist Association, which publishes a list of some 200 jewelers they recommend. Also contact the **DIAMOND IMPORTERS ASSOCIATION OF HONG KONG LTD.,** Diamond Exchange Building (Room 401), 8–10 Duddell Street,

Hong Kong, for their list of authorized agents. The Diamond Importers Association also publishes a variety of educational leaflets that you can send for ahead of your trip. Or call 523-5497 when you are in Hong Kong.

When looking for diamonds, judge their value by the four Cs—Cut, Clarity, Color, and Carat. The cut of the diamond is determined by your personal choice. No one cut is more valuable than others, although the round cut is the most classic and salable because it allows for the most brilliance and fire. Clarity in a diamond is judged by absence of inclusions, then number, size, and position of existing inclusions. A "flawless" diamond is unusual.

Color is an important factor in the value of the stone. A perfect blue-white stone is the most valuable. The more intense the color, the higher the price. Colorless diamonds are rare.

Carat is the weight of the stone. One carat equals ¼₀ gram. Price goes up as carat weight increases. There are 100 points per carat. A 4.02 carat stone would weigh 4 carats 2 points. A flawless stone larger than 1 carat is considered of investment quality because of its rarity.

Before you buy any stone get an independent appraisal done by the **GEMOLOGICAL LAB OF HONG KONG,** Luk Hoi Tong Building, 31 Queen's Road Central. It usually takes five working days to certify a diamond. It's worth the time to make sure that you don't get caught buying a cubic zirconia thinking it is a diamond.

Watches

Any type of watch you ever hoped to find is in Hong Kong. The trick is finding the right watch at the right price. You can pay anything from $50 to $10,000. If you are in the market for an international brand of watch, you are wisest to go to one of the authorized dealers for that brand. They are all listed in the phone book as well as through the Hong Kong Tourist Association. All of the companies expect to lower their prices by 10%. You might expect to get an even better discount if you pay in cash.

If you are looking to buy a fun, or interesting, watch, but don't care if it's a name brand, there are some things to be aware of before you buy:

▼ Check to see that the whole watch and not just the movement was made by the manufacturer. A common practice in Hong Kong is to sell a Swiss watch face and movement with a Hong Kong–made bracelet. The bracelet is probably silver with a gold plating. This can work to your advantage if you do not want to spend $5,000 for a solid-gold watch but want the look. A reputable dealer will tell you that this is what you are buying, and price the watch accordingly. These watches can cost anywhere from $150 to $400. We have found that you have the greatest bargaining power in this area, because the profit for the watchmaker is so high. On the other hand, dealers of name-brand watches have a limited play in their prices.

▼ Check the serial number on the inside movement with the serial number of your guarantee. If you do not receive a worldwide guarantee, don't buy the watch.

▼ If you are buying from a name-brand dealer, do the same careful checking as if you were buying from a small no-name shop on the street. We know of someone who bought a name-brand watch from a reputable dealer, got the watch home, and had problems. When she went to the U.S. dealer for that name, they told her that yes, indeed, she had bought one of their name watches, but the movement was five years old. She had bought a current body with a used movement!

▼ If it's not necessary that you find a name-brand watch, and you are simply looking for something unusual and fun, try the following:

CITY CHAIN: There is a particularly good branch of this popular chain at 16 Mody Road, Tsim Sha Tsui, Kowloon. City Chain carries Seiko, Bulova, and Zenith among their name brands. They also carry fashion watches like Smash (a takeoff of Swatch). There's a branch of this huge chain in every mall and shopping district.

SWATCH SHOP: 6 Great George Street, Causeway Bay, Hong Kong. Swatch is a big seller in Hong Kong. Prices are no cheaper than in the United States, but you might see some different styles.

For a list of authorized sole agents of big-time watchmakers and their phone numbers, see the back pages of the free HKTA booklet on shopping.

Cameras

Buying a camera in Hong Kong is confusing unless you are quite knowledgeable about the equipment and comparable prices. Every year there are new top-of-the-line models available in every brand, and they're all for sale in Hong Kong. Most shopkeepers will tout what they have in stock, and not necessarily what you need. Begin your search armed with the exact details of what it is you want. There is a Canon showroom in the Silvercord Building Arcade where you can test various models. You must supply your own film. Once you are quite sure of what you want, price-shop. Try several different stores and bargain as if you were going to buy. Don't buy, however, no matter how good the price seems. Wait and go back. If you got a good price the first time you will probably get it again. If you are buying a lot of equipment, ask for a larger discount. Take a copy of a recent ad from 47th Street Photo (these double-page ads run every Sunday in the *New York Times* and will give you an excellent reference for U.S. prices on cameras and other small electronic goods).

After you have decided where you are going to buy, insist on the following:

▼ Each piece of equipment needs its own (worldwide) warranty. The serial number of the piece must be clearly marked on the card, along with the agent's stamp and a complete address of where you purchased the item.

▼ Make sure you are not being charged for extras that should have been included in the original purchase. For example, camera cases usually come with the camera. You should not pay extra for the case.

▼ Watch your purchase being packed, and check each item as it goes into its box. Don't trust the store owner to pack and deliver your purchase to the hotel. When you get back you might discover that a few small items somehow got lost.

▼ Keep your receipts separate. Customs most likely will not want to open and go through all of your equipment if your receipts are clear and in order.

▼ For the name of an authorized importing agent for a name-brand camera, call the Consumer Council at 527-7662.

Our strongest recommendation for buying a camera comes from our friend Libby, who lived in Hong Kong and is a professional filmmaker. She depended on Mark's Photo

Supplies. There are a few other shops we liked as well:

MARK'S PHOTO SUPPLIES, 20 Des Voeux Road Central, Hong Kong. Steven Mark is the managing director of this shop, which has been in business for almost twenty years. It is not flashy or showy—as a matter of fact, it is not even very easy to find. Although the address is on Des Voeux Road Central, the entrance is actually on Theatre Lane.

ASIA PHOTO, 5 Queen Victoria Street, Hong Kong, and **CROWN PHOTO SUPPLIES LTD.,** 14 Queen Victoria Street, Hong Kong, are both large, well-stocked, convenient shops that cater to the tourist trade.

Computers and Small Electronic Devices

We have one important thing to say about buying computers: **ASIA COM-PUTER PLAZA,** in the basement of the Silvercord Building, 30 Canton Road, Kowloon, is the place to go to, to be safe. There are authorized dealers here for most of the big names in the computer world. There are bookstores (try **LEED & WOOD,** Shop 21) that sell programs and have information galore. We admit that the programs we priced offered no savings over U.S. discount prices. You can get fax machines, laptops, and type-writers with memories. The question is whether you want to or not. The big names like Apple, IBM, and NEC are sold at authorized stores in the East Asia Computer Plaza. You can haggle and bargain . . . possibly even make a good deal. Make sure, however, that the machine you buy is wired to work on the voltage where you will be using it. The Hong Kong voltage is 220, while standard voltage in the United States is 110. Don't let a salesperson convince you that a converter will do. Computers are much too sensitive, and you don't want to risk losing your program because of a power failure. Also make sure that the equipment you buy will work with the monitor you have at home.

If you are a little more adventurous, take the MTR to Sham Shui Po to visit the **GOLDEN ARCADE SHOPPING CENTRE,** 44B Fuk Wah Street. This area of Kowloon is very much a "real people" neighborhood, filled with street stalls selling blue jeans for $5, T-shirts, bed linens, ducks, and roosters. The street odor is strong. People are jammed into every nook and cranny of the area. In the midst of this craziness is the Golden Arcade Shopping Centre, a supermarket filled with computer hardware, software, and educational material. As you get out of the MTR you will be right there. . . . Just look up to see the arcade marquee. There is a directory listing all 120 shops, but it really doesn't matter. The only way to shop here is to wander and compare. Each shop has a different type of computer, and many if not most of them are clones. You have to know your equipment to shop successfully here. In the basement are software companies selling unofficial programs.

Important note: Take the time to open the package and run the program. One of our readers found that half the program would not boot. They ran a new copy for him on the spot. This is definitely a bargain-hard shopping environment.

Video Games

I f you are related in any way to a child under the age of 14, you are probably shopping for video games. Please see our expert's assessment of the Hong Kong Nintendo situation, on page 129.

Technologically speaking, the things a not-too-plugged-in parent needs to know are: Game Boy game cassettes are international in form, and they fit the U.S. and Asian machines interchangeably. We can't speak for the color version of Game Boy, which is promised for the future. Nintendo, on the other hand, has a Japanese system and an American system as well as a laser disc system (a whole other story, but a hot item to think about). Most of the Nintendo game cartridges sold in Hong Kong are for the Japanese system. However, you can buy a plastic converter for about $8. You only need one converter, although we have heard of some cases when the converter simply didn't work. So to be safe, we bought three; they all worked.

While local talent has not figured out how to bootleg American-style games, there are plenty of inexpensive Japanese versions on sale. The average price of an American game system is $45; a Japanese game is $30, and a bootleg copy can cost as little as $15. Game Boy cassettes sell for about $25 in the U.S. and $15–$20 in Hong Kong. Prices should be negotiable according to how many you buy. They do sell some Nintendo products at the Hong Kong airport.

Most camera and/or small electronics stores sell video games. Japanese department stores have huge selections of games (your kids do not care if the instructions are written in Japanese), but prices tend to be slightly higher than at camera shops. Japanese department stores do sell all versions of the games, including the newer laser disc system.

If you are looking to buy game programs for a PC, shop very carefully. We priced "Where in the World Is Carmen Sandiego?" and found Hong Kong to be more expensive than home.

Our two best sources for video games are: **MASSKEY DEVELOPMENT LTD.,** Golden Building, 152 Fuk Wah Street, Sham Shui Po, Kowloon; and **RICKY LAU,** Haiphong Alley, Kowloon. For Nintendo games (Japanese-style) we pay $25 tops; for Sega games we pay about one half the U.S. price.

Optical Goods

In the olden days, Hong Kong was a bonanza of inexpensive eyeglass frames, optical care, and contact lenses. No more. While you can still find inexpensive frames in the $30–$50 range, a completed pair of glasses is likely to cost you the same thing as what you pay at home at your favorite chain or discount service center. And if anything goes wrong at home, you can return to the shop and have it fixed.

Prices for contact lenses were identical to what we pay in the U.S.

Fabrics and Notions

As one of the ready-to-wear manufacturing capitals of the world, Hong Kong has more fabrics and notions than just about any other city we've seen. Prices for even the most luscious Chinese or Japanese silks are reasonable—although Chinese silk is much less expensive than Japanese. (Japanese silks are much more intricately printed; the Chinese rarely run multiple screens on their silks.)

There are two basic fabrics and notions neighborhoods: Jardine's Bazaar and the Lanes. When you go to Jardine's Bazaar weave in and around all the little streets behind the market itself; you'll find numerous fabrics, notions, and yarn shops with incredibly low prices.

Wool and synthetic wool yarns are very inexpensive in Hong Kong. You'll find some excellent knitting shops in the Lanes, and there are several in Causeway Bay.

You can buy fabrics from most tailors; there's a large selection of Chinese silks in all Chinese Arts & Crafts Stores. A nice silk runs about $25 per yard. This happens to be the same price we pay in New York. Bespoke tailors always have a large selection of fabrics for men's suits and shirts, but you cannot buy these goods off the bolt. For the truly fashion-conscious woman, it might be easier to bring fabrics from home.

Raw silk is available at most Chinese department stores and costs about $15 a yard. This is comparable to the U.S. price, but the color selection may be better in Hong Kong. Brides, note: White-and-cream raw silk gowns are "in" (in the U.S.). You can indeed have a wedding gown made in Hong Kong.

And of course **WING ON STREET** is not called Cloth Alley because it sells cameras! Wing On Street is near Western Market in Central.

Embroidery and Whitework

The Chinese are famous for their embroidery. One variety that we particularly like is done on linen or cotton, by machine and hand, and we refer to it as "whitework," which is actually a Victorian name describing the white-on-white variety. Antique embroidered goods are quite valuable. Tablecloths, napkins, place mats, sweaters, jackets, and fabric purses are all sold with embroidery. The best drawn embroidery is supposed to come from Swatow in China.

Since more and more of our friends are becoming collectors of whitework, we get requests to bring it back from all over the world. We shopped in Spain and Portugal for embroidered goods and were surprised to find a lot of Chinese imports there. Be careful to learn the look of hand embroidery versus machine embroidery. Most of the shop goods are machine-made. Hand embroidery is very expensive. If you want finely crafted pieces try:

HANDART EMBROIDERIES, Hing Wai Building, 36 Queen's Road Central, Hong Kong. This shop offers a particularly good selection of bed linens, place mats, and doilies.

THE CHINESE BAZAAR, Prince's Building, Chater Road, Hong Kong. This store offers a good selection in table linens, napkins, coasters, and children's clothing. They have been in business since 1905.

LACE LANE, Silvercord Building, Canton Road, Kowloon, and Wing On Plaza, 62 Mody Road, Tsim Sha Tsui East, Kowloon. These two shops are our favorites for selection, and service. The hand-smocked dresses for little girls are especially wonderful. They will special-order for you.

WAH SING LACE COMPANY, 7 On Lan Street, Hong Kong. On Lan Street is a short block full of wholesalers and manufacturers. Not all may offer retail, but this is a good lane for finding bargains. Wah Sing manufactures and does export, in case you want to buy lots.

KAI WAH HANDICRAFT, Sheraton Hotel Shopping Arcade, Salisbury Road, Kowloon, is a seemingly typical little shop no different from a zillion others. We found the help lacking in manners and unwilling to bargain or deal in any way. Yet we keep returning to buy because of the selection and styles we can't find elsewhere. If you want whitework that is not duded up with flowers and too much embroidery; if you like simple and plain but very nice—this is one of the few sources where you can find it. Also note the Christmas ornaments: For $10 you get a box of four needlepoint old-fashiony Father Christmas figures (each different) made in the British tradition.

Please note that good drawnwork is getting harder and harder to find. Young people don't want to do it (wrecks the eyes) and shipment/business procedures from China are dicey, so orders don't come in when anticipated. If you find the real thing, expect to pay dearly for it. Once you have seen finely made, handbound cutwork or drawnwork you will laugh at what is generally sold in markets, Chinese department stores, and crafts stores. Also please see our Bed N Bath Rule of Shopping (page 9), because you may find mass-produced whitework in the U.S. for less than it costs in Hong Kong.

It's very hard to quote prices and remain accurate as the world turns, but we admit that in almost all cases we thought prices for whitework and embroidery in Hong Kong were expensive, especially when compared to the quality we were offered. Expect to pay about

$25–$35 for a set of four place mats with napkins. The higher price is for more details, cuts, or embroidery.

Needlepoint

One of our great disappointments is that so far we cannot find a source for those fabulous country and quasi-French needlepoint pillows that we all know are coming out of China. Since these cost about $80 as finished pillows in the U.S., we would expect them to be quite affordable in Hong Kong, and would happily buy them even if they were not made up into throw pillows. Alas, the Chinese department stores all have a counter devoted to finished needlepoint canvas scenes, but we are talking styles and designs that are only slightly classier than a portrait of Elvis painted on black velvet. You might luck into the Last Supper, but you will not find florals or anything pretty.

We are also still looking for someone who will finish all the needlepoints we have started and left half done. If someone can make a suit in three days, someone else should be able to finish a pillow. Stay tuned.

Cosmetics and Fragrances

Cosmetics and fragrances are not as inexpensive in Hong Kong as in Paris, but may be less than in the United States. They can also be more. The best thing is that scents that have been introduced in Europe, but not in the United States, are available in Hong Kong. So if you want to sniff out the latest, Hong Kong offers you that opportunity.

We have comparison-shopped all the big department stores—British, Japanese, Chinese, you name it—and we find that they all have pretty much the same prices. We buy what we need but prefer to mail-order from Catherine in Paris.

Take note: Major big-name cosmetics companies manufacture for the Far East in and around Hong Kong; often they will have a product with the same name as the product you use at home, but it will be slightly different. They may also have a product, or shade, that you will have never heard of and will never find again anywhere else in the world.

Another note: The large duty-free shop at the airport is well stocked and easy to shop.

FANDA PERFUME COMPANY, 21 Lock Road, Kowloon; World Wide Plaza, Pedder Street, Hong Kong; Houston Centre, Tsim Sha Tsui East, Kowloon. Lily and her friends all buy their perfumes and cosmetics at this convenient shop, where prices are discounted on many items, including Badedas.

THE BODY SHOP, The Landmark, Gloucester Tower, 16 Des Voeux Road Central, Hong Kong, or The Mall at Pacific Place, 88 Queensway, Hong Kong. We love this English natural cosmetics line that has taken the United States and Hong Kong by storm. All the products come in biodegradable containers and are made from natural ingredients. There is a complete line of cosmetics as well as soaps with scents like sandalwood and jasmine. Treat yourself to a bottle of Peppermint Foot Massage Creme after a hard day of bargain hunting. No savings.

SHU UEMURA, The Landmark, 16 Des Voeux Road Central, Hong Kong, and Harbour City/Ocean Centre, 5 Canton Road, Kowloon. We first discovered this line of cosmetics and skin-care products in Tokyo, then in Paris, L.A., New York, and now Hong Kong. Nobody does better colors in eyeshadow. Makeup junkies shouldn't miss the opportunity.

China and Crystal

The largest china and crystal stores are in or near the major hotels and shopping centers. They all ship and take orders from overseas. The only problem arises when the store is out of stock. You can have many dinner parties before your missing pieces arrive. Check on availability before you place your order. European lines stocked locally include Royal Crown Derby, Royal Albert Spode, Royal Brierley, Royal Worcester, Hammersley, Edinburgh, Robbs and Berking, Royal Minton, Royal Doulton, Lladró, Limoges, Herend, Ginori, Saint Louis, Boehm, Rosenthal, Baccarat, Lalique, and Wedgwood.

While you may save on pieces you can carry yourself, once you ship you wipe out any big savings.

BACCARAT, The Landmark, Gloucester Tower, 16 Des Voeux Road Central, Hong Kong

CRAIG'S, St. George's Building, 2 Ice House Street, Hong Kong (next to the Mandarin Oriental Hotel); Harbour City/Ocean Centre, 5 Canton Road, Kowloon

GRENLEY'S, Swire House, Connaught Road Central, Hong Kong

HUNTER'S, The Peninsula Hotel, Salisbury Road, Kowloon; Harbour City/Ocean Terminal, Canton Road, Kowloon; Kowloon Hotel, 19–21 Nathan Road, Kowloon; Repulse Bay, 109 Repulse Bay Road, Repulse Bay,

Hong Kong; The Mall at Pacific Place, 88 Queensway, Hong Kong (MTR: Admiralty)

EILEEN KERSHAW, The Peninsula Hotel, Salisbury Road, Kowloon; The Landmark, 16 Des Voeux Road Central, Hong Kong

LLADRÓ, The Peninsula Hotel, Salisbury Road, Kowloon; Alexandra House, Des Voeux Road Central, Hong Kong

ROSENTHAL, Prince's Building, Chater Road, Hong Kong

ROYAL COPENHAGEN, Prince's Building, Chater Road, Hong Kong; Harbour City/Ocean Terminal, Canton Road, Kowloon

WATERFORD/WEDGWOOD, The Landmark, Gloucester Tower, 16 Des Voeux Road Central, Hong Kong

Chinese China also is available, and there are many outlets. One of the easiest sources for vases and tea sets is the Chinese department stores. We like **CHINESE ARTS & CRAFTS,** in either of their stores, at Star House or the Silvercord Building, Kowloon. Also in Kowloon, try **CHUNG KIU CHINESE PRODUCTS EMPORIUM LTD.,** 17 Hankow Road, or **YUE HWA,** Park Lane Shopper's Arcade, Nathan Road.

Chinese porcelain factories are a popular shopper's attraction—you can see some of the goods in production if you catch a good day. The factories are not easy or convenient to get to, so we suggest that you plan your day around the visit, leave plenty of time, and remember that most factories close for lunch, usually between 1 P.M. and 2 P.M. Also remember public holidays when factories close (see page 32). One of our favorite factory outlets for Chinese porcelains is **AH CHOW FACTORY,** Hong Kong Industrial Centre, 489 Castle Peak Road, Kowloon (MTR: Lai Chi Kok). We also like **WAH TUNG CHINA COMPANY,** Grand Marine Industrial Building, 3 Yue Fung Street, Tin Wan, Aberdeen, Hong Kong. You have to take a taxi here, or a car, but you can have lunch in Aberdeen. This is the single largest source for

Chinese porcelain in Hong Kong. They will send a van to pick you up. We rate this as a four-star shopping dream.

Chops (And We Don't Mean Lamb)

O f course we know what a chop is. It's served for dinner and comes in the pork, veal, or lamb category. Or so we thought.

It turns out that in China, a chop is a form of signature stamp (not made of rubber) on which a symbol for a person's name is carved. The chop is dipped in dry dye (instead of an ink pad) and then placed on paper to create a signature stamp—much like a rubber stamp.

The main difference between rubber stamps and chops is that rubber stamps were invented after the Bessemer process and became trendy only in the early 1980s, whereas chops were invented about 2,200 years ago.

Since chops go so far back, you can choose from an antique or a newly created version. Antiques are quite pricey, depending on age, importance of the carving, materials used, and maybe even the autograph that is engraved. New chops have little historic importance but make great gifts.

Although chops vary in size, they are traditionally the size of a chessman, with a square or round base. Up to four Chinese characters or three Western initials can be inscribed on the base.

The quality of a chop varies greatly, based on the ability of the person who does the carving. We have done enough chop shopping to know that the very best place to get a chop is in Man Wa Lane. But every hotel has at least one gift shop that will have your chop engraved. (You must allow at least twenty-four hours.) While prices vary on chops, obviously, we paid $20 for a fabulous one—midsize but brilliantly carved.

You can buy little pots of the proper dye in any gift shop ($1) or use a regular old ink pad. Red is the color for your true love's chop ink.

Arts, Crafts, and Antiques

Hunting down bargains in arts, crafts, and antiques is one of our favorite shopping adventures in Hong Kong. Our definition of arts and crafts is broad enough to include handwork of any kind, from hand-carved teaware to cloisonné that has been done within the last 100 years. We include pottery that is original or copies of originals, ivory carvings, jade carvings, handmade dolls, and papercuts. The how and why of some of these subjects we tackle in Chapter 5. The where to get them is not so precise a topic. Antiques are often arts and crafts that are over 100 years old. Some of our sources carry antiques and arts and crafts. Some just carry fun crafts. Some just carry antiques.

A good way to get a fix on the arts, crafts, and antiques of China is to begin with a visit to some of Hong Kong's museums:

HONG KONG MUSEUM OF ART, High Block, City Hall (10th and 11th floors), Hong Kong, has a collection of 2,800 antiquities, including ceramics, bronzes, cloisonné, snuff bottles, papercuts, and embroidery. Paintings and calligraphy dating from the 17th to the 20th centuries are represented as well. Educational material is available, and there is a gift shop with replicas and postcards. This museum is closed on Thursday. Other days it is open 10 A.M. to 6 P.M., and on Sunday, 1 P.M. to 6 P.M.

FLAGSTAFF HOUSE MUSEUM OF TEA WARE, Victoria Barracks (enter from Cotton Tree Drive), Hong Kong, is a branch of the Hong Kong Museum of Art. It is housed in the oldest Western-style building left in Hong Kong. There are 560 pieces of teaware, mainly Chinese, with a good selection of Yixing teapots. The museum is closed Wednesday and open 10 A.M. to 5 P.M. every other day. Taxi here.

We feel that arts and crafts and antiques are wonderful buys. It is hard to comparison-shop for them, because you never see two things of the same kind. If you do, you shouldn't be buying them anyway.

The Hong Kong Tourist Association publishes a list of factories that produce brassware, carpets, carved furniture, Chinese lanterns, pewter, and china and are open to the public.

For the ultimate thrill in antiques collecting, frequent the auction galleries. Auctions are advertised in the *South China Morning Post.* Large auctions of priceless porcelains make front-page news. If you wish advance notice or catalogues before you visit, write to:

ASSOCIATED FINE ARTS AUCTIONEERS, LTD., Entertainment Building (13th floor), 30 Queen's Road Central, Hong Kong (telephone: 522-2088)

CHRISTIE MANSON & WOODS LTD., Alexandra House, Des Voeux Road Central, Hong Kong (telephone: 521-5396)

LAMMERT BROTHERS, 10 Stanley Street (9th floor), Hong Kong (telephone: 522-3208)

SOTHEBY'S H.K. LTD., Lane Crawford House, Queen's Road Central, Hong Kong (telephone: 524-8121)

Arts and Crafts

EILEEN KERSHAW: This shop, in The Peninsula Hotel, is on the upper end of fine arts and crafts stores. Their business card is a three-way foldout with the Chinese dynasties listed along the entire back half. The front has a list of birthstones, in case you want to buy a present for a friend, as well as a place for notes on what you have seen.

The shop is extremely large, but seems less so because there are pieces of stonework, display cases, packing crates, and porcelain jars everywhere you look. The sales help is very understanding and pleasant. Prices are average. The antique vases are displayed on the highest shelves, so that curious travelers cannot touch. Antique paintings, china, carpets, and wall hangings are a large part of the store's business, but do not involve the usual walk-in tourist. If you are interested in a special type of item, ask. The store will do mail-order as well.

EILEEN KERSHAW, The Peninsula Hotel, Salisbury Road, Kowloon

▼

AMAZING GRACE ELEPHANT COMPANY: Amazing Grace carries handcrafted items from all over Asia. In particular we like the Taiwanese temple carvings. You can also buy silk pillow covers, brass carts, bowls, candlesticks, incense burners, jewelry, Korean chests, paper carvings, fans, dolls, bird cages, mirror frames, tea sets, and more. This shop has a broad appeal and can be a good source for small, inexpensive gift items. Branch stores are as far away as Sha Tui or as near as the Excelsior Hotel in Causeway Bay.

The warehouse/outlet, in the New Territories, is open to the public. If you are doing serious shopping it might be worth the drive.

You cannot get there any other way but by car, so take that into consideration. We suggest you stop in the Harbour City/Ocean Terminal shop and get directions. This is a warehouse situation, so be prepared. Wholesale prices are predicated on how much you buy, or on the cost of the goods. You can save a small fortune—and spend one too.

AMAZING GRACE ELEPHANT COMPANY, Harbour City/Ocean Terminal, Canton Road, Kowloon

AMAZING GRACE OUTLET, Yeu Shing Industrial Building, 4 Kin Fung Street, Tuen Mun, New Territories (telephone: 463-8156)

▼

YUE KEE CURIO COMPANY: Yue Kee has many options in fine art curios, including carvings, wall pieces, floor pieces, screens, and statues. There are also Chinese vases in every size. The shop is very crowded, and we don't suggest that you bring children or large shopping bags. It will take some time to make your mind up here. Yue Kee also has antiques.

YUE KEE CURIO COMPANY, Omni The Hong Kong Hotel Arcade, Harbour City, 2 Canton Road, Kowloon

▼

MOUNTAIN FOLKCRAFT: One of our favorite shops for handcrafted items, Mountain Folkcraft carries a little bit of everything in a small amount of space. When you go into the shop, shed your coat and bags at the door, because you are going to need room to stoop, bend, and sift through the items that are displayed, in order to see the ones below. We love their dolls, papercuts, woodblock prints, antique fabric pieces, batik fabric, boxes, chests, puppets, baskets, toys, and pottery.

MOUNTAIN FOLKCRAFT, Harbour City/Ocean Terminal, Lantao Gallery, Canton Road, Kowloon

▼

BANYAN TREE LTD.: Banyan Tree is a mass-market kind of handicrafts shop that sells rattan furniture, fabrics, figurines, lamps, porcelains, rugs, screens, and hundreds of other items for the home on both a retail and wholesale basis. They have a large exporting business, and can deliver anything you buy to your hometown. We would trust Banyan Tree to pack and ship anything. This is sort of the local Pier 1.

BANYAN TREE LTD.
Harbour City/Ocean Galleries, 25–27 Canton Road, Kowloon
Prince's Building, Chater Road, Hong Kong

▼

CHUNG KIU CHINESE PRODUCTS EMPORIUM: This smallish department store inside the Sands Building in Tsim Sha Tsui has four floors, three of which are devoted to handicrafts products. On the main floor look for jade, cloisonné, ivory, and semiprecious stone carvings. Upstairs there is jewelry, embroidery, silk, and tailoring. For Chinese carpets go to the 4th floor. This place is a dump, but great fun.

CHUNG KIU CHINESE PRODUCTS EMPORIUM, Sands Building, 17 Hankow Road, Kowloon

▼

ORIENTAL ARTS & JEWELLERY COMPANY: Oriental Arts & Jewellery is an importing company located on the 3rd floor of a Nathan Road office building near the Park Lane Shopper's Boulevard.

Go around the corner to find the entrance, take a rickety elevator, step over straw in the hall, and look for the red door that says "A." Come prepared to stay, because this is arts and crafts nirvana. As you walk into the room you see warehouse-type display racks in front of you. On them are a variety of vases, cloisonné items, porcelain, and stone carvings in jade and lapis. Behind and to the side are crates and more crates. Some have their tops opened; some have not yet been touched. The shipments are, for the most part, from mainland Chinese factories. On our tour through mainland China a few years before, we visited factories where cloisonné work was done. The factories all had shops. The prices here were cheaper for the same size vase, two years later. (A 6″ vase was $20.) The imports are mostly new copies of old pieces. However, there are also some old pieces that are offered for sale. One Chinese couple who were there when we came in sat for the entire hour we were there negotiating the price of a 3′ lavender jade carving. This shop is magnificent and one of our best Hong Kong finds. George Chan is the owner.

ORIENTAL ARTS & JEWELLERY COMPANY, 80 Nathan Road, Kowloon

▼

WAH TUNG CHINA COMPANY: One of the largest antiques reproduction facilities for china in Hong Kong and a must-do for china freaks. Wah Tung produces plain white porcelain in various shapes and sizes, including large jardinieres and small vases. Their craftspeople handpaint each piece in the tradition of a period or style. The factory and the showroom are enormous. They take special orders from individuals, decorators, or stores. Custom dinnerware is also available. Take a taxi. They ship. Or call for the van. Take the elevator.

WAH TUNG CHINA COMPANY, Grand Marine Industrial Building, 3 Yue Fung Street, Tin Wan, Aberdeen, Hong Kong

▼

TAI PING CARPETS: One of the major crafts industries in China is carpet-making. Carpets are still made by hand, and many take years to complete. Tai Ping is one of the leading manufacturers and importers. You can visit their retail shop and order a custom carpet (takes 6–12 weeks), or check out the factory shop on Monday and Thursday from 2 P.M. to 4 P.M. In Hong Kong call 656-5161, ext. 211, to arrange the visit.

TAI PING CARPETS
  Hutchison House, 10 Harcourt Road, Hong Kong
  Wing On Plaza, Mody Road, Kowloon
FACTORY SHOP
  Tai Ping Industrial Park, Ting Kok Road, Lot No. 1687, Tai Po Market, New Territories

Art and Antiques

We have a minimal section on art and antiques for several reasons:

▼ The bulk of the internationally famous dealers in Asian art are in London, New York, Tokyo, Brussels, and places other than Hong Kong.

▼ The amount of fakes and frauds in the art business is infamous. The situation is even more intense in Hong Kong, and in no way can we confirm the authenticity of your purchase.

▼ The antiques scene in Hong Kong is shifting. Some dealers are moving away from Hollywood Road; others have now set up in Antique Row in Harbour City/Ocean Galleries (3rd floor), which makes them not only more accessible to tourists but less shady looking.

We remind you to buy what you know; if you don't know much, buy what you love regardless of its real value. Bring your own expert with you if you are truly serious, or hire one in Hong Kong. A magazine called *Orientations* is available in Hong Kong—it's much like *Connoisseur*—and may help you with news and prices. There are also a number of big-time auctions in Hong Kong; both Sotheby's and Christie's have offices here. Auctions are held in either spring or fall.

LUEN CHAI CURIOS STORE: These are curios like we're Minnie Mouse—this Cat Street dealer has scrolls, antique porcelain, and exhibition space to show contemporary Chinese painting.

LUEN CHAI CURIOS STORE
   22 Upper Lascar Row, Hong Kong
   142 Hollywood Road, Hong Kong

▼

HANART GALLERY: One of the most famous galleries in the world for scrolls. Their exhibition space often represents modern Chinese art. This is the place to go, to know, to be known, to be in. Their reputation is outstanding. They also have galleries in New York and Taipei.

HANART GALLERY, 40 Hollywood Road, Hong Kong

▼

C. P. CHING: Art and objets d'art from all over the Orient, so that only a portion of the selection is Chinese, but all of it is serious and expensive.

C. P. CHING SHOP I: 21 Hollywood Road, Hong Kong

C. P. CHING SHOP II: The Mall at Pacific Place, 88 Queensway, Hong Kong (MTR: Admiralty)

▼

TAI SING CO.: Since 1957 a leading dealer in important Han, T'ang, and Sung porcelains, as well as Imperial porcelain, which is outrageously expensive. They also sell Chinese export porcelain. (This, too, is expensive.)

TAI SING CO., 122 Hollywood Road, Hong Kong

▼

PLUM BLOSSOM INT'L LTD.: While we are not much on contemporary Chinese painting, we have actually seen work at Plum Blossom that we like. But what we really love is their selection of antique textile arts and Tibetan carpets. This is the kind of place you can look to for guidance in the area of expensive items that will accrue in value. Exchange Square is downtown, near the Mandarin Oriental Hotel.

PLUM BLOSSOM INT'L LTD., Exchange Square, Hong Kong (MTR: Central)

▼

MARTIN FUNG ANTIQUES AND FURNITURE COMPANY: At the far end of Hollywood Road are the Cat Street Galleries and Martin Fung's showroom. Most of the stock in this two-level shop is lacquer furniture. However, the variety is enormous. You can get antique lacquer chests or boxes, or new ones. There are complete living room, dining room, and bedroom sets. Martin Fung deals mainly with decorators and store buyers, but will sell and ship to anyone. If you are placing a large order, talk wholesale.

MARTIN FUNG ANTIQUES AND FURNITURE COMPANY, Cat Street Galleries (1st floor), 38 Lok Ku Road, Hong Kong

▼

P. C. LU & SONS LTD.: A fine antiques dealer with showrooms in the major hotels, P. C. Lu's family has been in the business for four generations and runs one of the finest resources for antique ivory and jade, porcelain, and decorative work. The three sons, who now run the business, work closely together. Stop in at any of the galleries and browse.

P. C. LU & SONS LTD., The Peninsula Hotel, Salisbury Road, Kowloon

▼

CHARLOTTE HORSTMANN & GERALD GODFREY LTD.: One of the most popular and well-respected antiques shops in Hong Kong, Charlotte Horstmann and Gerald Godfrey offer a wide range in museum-class Asian antiques. There are pieces from Korea, Burma, China, Japan, Indonesia, and India. Choices include *Noh* masks, Chinese scrolls, Ming tapestries, T'ang horses, and period furniture made of sandalwood, rosewood, and blackwood. It has been rumored that the shop may move from Ocean Terminal. But they were there the last time we were.

CHARLOTTE HORSTMANN & GERALD GODFREY LTD., Harbour City/Ocean Terminal, Canton Road, Kowloon

JADE HOUSE: Small but impressive, Jade House has been run by members of the C. K. Liang family for five generations. Mr. Liang's personal collection of early jade is magnificent. The shop specializes in antique jadeite and nephrite, as well as snuff bottles. There is another branch in the Kowloon Hotel.

JADE HOUSE, 1-D Mody Road, Kowloon
C. K. LIANG & SONS, Kowloon Hotel, 19–21 Nathan Road, Kowloon

▼

HONEYCHURCH ANTIQUES: Located on Hollywood Road, Honeychurch deserves to be singled out for its quality and honesty. Glenn and Lucille Vessa are the owners, and they are extremely knowledgeable in the ways of antiques. Their store carries a wide variety of merchandise and they are always willing to give advice on where to go if you have a special need. The look is sort of Oriental Country.

HONEYCHURCH ANTIQUES, 29 Hollywood Road, Hong Kong

8 ▼ TOURS, DAY TRIPS, AND DETOURS

Hong Kong on a Schedule

There are no listings here that have not been mentioned elsewhere, but the details or directions might be more explicit in this chapter. If you don't know your way around Hong Kong and do not have a car and driver, we think you should try one or two of our tours. With the average stay in Hong Kong a mere three days, you need to see (and shop) as much as possible. Our tours cram it all in.

Tour 1: Hong Kong—Central and Sane

Your first day in Hong Kong should be easy and fun. The Hong Kong side, especially Central District, is the most understandable place to start. This is the area where all of the large shopping centers, as well as the majority of office buildings, are located.

1. If you are staying in Kowloon, come across the harbor on the Star Ferry. This is the best way to view Central for the first time, as the skyline is spectacular. Crossing under Connaught Road Central on the pedestrian walkway will bring you up between Statue Square and the Mandarin Oriental Hotel.

2. The Mandarin Oriental Hotel is home to two of the most popular tailor shops in town. On the mezzanine level you will find

David's (shirts) and A-Man (suits). Also on the mezzanine don't miss the jewelry shop, Gemsland.

3. There are numerous designer boutiques as well. You might want to begin the day with a power breakfast in The Grill. Leave the hotel via the pedestrian bridge that connects the Mandarin Oriental to the Prince's Building across the street. Explore many levels of designer shops.

4. After leaving the Prince's Building, cross the street and walk to Swire House (in the middle of the block and before you get to Pedder Street). Swire House is a perfect example of an office building/shopping center. Within the Swire House arcade, you will find numerous designer boutiques.

5. Leave Swire House via the Chater Road exit, take a right, and then an immediate left onto Des Voeux Road Central, where you will be in front of The Landmark. Enter The Landmark after visiting Hermès (entrance on the street) and Dickson Watch & Jewellery Co. Ltd. (also on the street). One entrance into the building is beside Gucci. Walk past Gucci, down a somewhat claustrophobic hallway, toward the throngs of people and center atrium. Once in the atrium, spend some time gawking like the rest of the tourists. We gawk every time we visit The Landmark. The biggest names in design are here. If you are looking for discount shopping only, don't waste your time. . . . Move on, or grab a bite to eat. However, if you are not going to Europe soon and want to purchase expensive fashions from the top designer houses, start shopping. In The Landmark you will find Céline, Lanvin, Cacharel, Krizia, Ellesse, Jaeger, Versace, Ferré, Vuitton, Gucci, Courrèges, Ungaro, Montana, etc., and a score of other shops. The Landmark could be an all-day adventure in itself.

6. Exit The Landmark via the Pedder Street door, cross at the corner of Queen's Road Central, turn right down Pedder Street, and look for the Pedder Building (No. 12: a small entryway right next to the China Building). If you get to the Mandarin House, you have gone too far. The building is a dump. The spaces now occupied by designer boutiques were once, not so long ago, workrooms. The boutiques are nice but the hallways are not.

7. If you still have the energy at this point to go on, exit the Pedder Building, take a right, and then another right onto Queen's Road Central. Stay on the harbor side of the street and walk in the direction of Pottinger Street.

8. As you walk along Queen's Road Central in the westerly direction, stop for a spree in the Lanes, which are located before Pottinger Street. You'll pass Dragon Seed (No. 39), a Chinese department store that will intrigue bargain and junk shoppers and soon get to the Lanes, with Li Yuen Street East coming before Li Yuen West (unless you are very lost). Walk to your right, going down Li Yuen Street East and shopping your heart out until you get to Des Voeux Road, then walk the few yards it takes to get to Li Yuen West on Des Voeux, turn to your left into the lane, walking back to Queen's Road Central along a shopping lane similar to the one you were just on. While you may not need a brassiere, do note that souvenir T-shirts cost only a little more than $1 and Hermès-style Kelly handbags cost less than $50.

9. Your last stop of the day should be the Lane Crawford Department Store, across the street from Mandarin Optical and farther toward Pottinger Street. Here you can find a sampling of anything you want, from truly fine art to portrait photography, from

china and crystal to Mikimoto pearls. You can even get a pedicure for your very tired feet at Elizabeth Arden.

10. Taxi back to your hotel with all of your packages. If you like night markets and still haven't had enough adventure (you're our kind of person), make reservations for an early dinner and plan to be at the Temple Street Market at about 9 P.M. This is a very hot night market in Kowloon, where Chinese opera is performed in the streets.

Tour 2: Hong Kong Adventure

It is possible to be in Hong Kong and not experience the flavor of this exciting, energetic city. If you visit only Central, your view will be that Hong Kong is a very civilized, clean, modern, disciplined city. However, the real Hong Kong is more than just shopping centers, luxury hotels, and large office compounds. The street life is what makes the city vibrate. This adventure is for the person who enjoys the sensuous aspects of a city—and we don't mean the red-light district!

Put on your walking shoes and bring your umbrella (useful as both a parasol and a walking stick). Get ready to experience Hong Kong.

1. Begin your day at the foot of Pottinger Street, next to the China Products Store on Queen's Road Central. Pottinger is a very steep street with scads of stalls and an equal number of steps. The stalls have very diverse merchandise, including handbags, clothing, and food.

If you are truly an adventurous soul and like all kinds of markets, before you climb Pottinger Street go farther along Queen's Road Central (away from Lane Crawford), to the large Central Market. This is the source of much of the produce purchased by restaurants and hotels. Here you will see an amazing range of Chinese fruits, vegetables, and, of course, fresh meat . . . very fresh!

2. When you make it to the top of Pottinger Street you will be at the crossroads of Chinese antiques and curios heaven—better known as Hollywood Road. Hollywood Road became popular in the early 1950s, after the Revolution in China. At that time many Chinese had fled the People's Republic with possessions in hand. In order to raise cash, they pawned them on Hollywood Road. The tradition remained, and Hollywood Road is still the center of merchandise coming out of China. Most of what you see in the shops today is not antique but antique repro. The true finds are in the back rooms and are saved for dealers. However, if you are an antiques collector, let the shop owner know immediately upon entering the store that you are in the market for fine pieces and are willing to deal. Often it is better to have an introduction to a dealer in town who can shop and negotiate with you. For the majority of shoppers, who want a curio to take home, rummaging through dusty shelves for the "perfect" piece is a lot of fun! Just remember that there are no Ming vases on the shelves. Ask lots of questions, and bargain. Try to pay cash, as credit cards often add 4% to your bill. Make sure you get a receipt stating the age of your purchase. If you are buying a true antique you are entitled to a certificate of authenticity. Customs will want to see these papers. In the more established shops, shipping is no problem and the goods arrive safely. If you are planning to buy in quantity for any reason, ask for the dealer price. Bring along your business card and negotiate on a quantity basis. Many of the shops are used to dealing

with interior designers who buy for their clients.

Hollywood Road is actually an extension of Wyndham Street, with stores running right to the block after the Man Mo Temple. The closer you get to Ladder Street, the tackier the shops become. After the temple the shops become a mix of Chinese herbalists, furniture makers, and curio stores. Be sure to go into a Chinese medicine shop and look at all the wonderful, exotic substances in glass jars. The wizened old men concocting remedies for any ailment you might have probably are the only true antiques left on Hollywood Road.

3. At this point you will have passed the Man Mo Temple. If you didn't go into this shrine, do so. There is nothing to buy, except a Coca-Cola from a stand at the corner, but the experience is important for an understanding of Chinese life. The burning incense, filtered light, larger-than-life statues, smoke-filled rooms, and candles all contribute to a visual sense of the Chinese lifestyle.

4. Exit the temple and go to the corner of Hollywood Road and Ladder Street. Ladder Street is another of those wonderful stepped streets that looks like it has been there for centuries. Most of the street actually runs uphill, but you will be thrilled to know that you will be going downhill. Pass by the street hawkers selling jade, go to Cat Street (also known as Upper Lascar Road), and turn left. This is a really fun street to walk and shop for junk. Vendors have not set up stalls. All the merchandise is displayed on blankets laid on the ground. Each vendor specializes in a different variety of "junk." Farther along the street you will see workshops making furniture and forging metals. Dealers who sell mostly to the design trade have their showrooms in the Cat Street Galleries, which is in the middle of the block,

in the Casey Building on the harbor side of the street. The actual address for the gallery is on the next street down the hill, so if you miss the building on Cat Street, walk to the end of Cat Street, turn right, duck under the hanging laundry, and turn right again on Lok Ku Road.

5. If you have the energy to walk, go down the steps of Ladder Street to Man Wah Lane, taking Hillier Road. If you can't walk, you can almost roll. Man Wah Lane is the only place to buy a chop and is also the best place to have your business cards made up in Chinese (a great gift for the person who has everything).

6. If you have strength for one more adventure, walk the few extra blocks to Wing Lok, which runs parallel to Bonham Strand East. This neighborhood is very Chinese and not touristy or Western. Explore to your heart's content. Then pop into the Sheung Wan MTR station and head home.

Tour 3: Half-Day Adventures—Yet More Bargains (Includes Stanley Market)

These two tours are at opposite ends of the Hong Kong world, so divide them in half by lunch, or separate them into two different days if you have time. We suggest lunch in or near your hotel, because you'll want to make a pit stop to drop off your packages.

1. Take a taxi to Hung Hom; ask for Kaiser Estates Phase II. Explore the many factory outlets in the area (see page 98), then call for a cab if you don't see one on the streets. The showroom at Made in Hong Kong will call for you.

2. Stanley Market. Take the bus or a taxi to Stanley Market in the afternoon. Look out

the windows to get a bird's-eye view of the
real Hong Kong. See page 137 for directions
to and suggestions for Stanley Market. Despite the fact that this market may offer no
steals, we still believe in it and urge you to
go, if you have the time.

Tour 4: Kowloon—All-Day Bargain/Treasure Hunting: Outlets, Markets, Hot Young Designer Boutiques, and All That Stuff

Kowloon has many different shopping areas,
each of which should be a day's adventure. In
our one-day tour we will cover only our favorites; there are many more in our listings. And
you will have no trouble finding adventures
of your own, no matter where you wander.
Begin your day early. The shops all open by
9:30 A.M., and you should be at our first shop
at that time. Our second stop is a market that
opens at 10 A.M. and closes around noon, so
judge your time accordingly.

1. If you are staying in Kowloon, walk to the
   Ocean Terminal, just to the right of the Star
   Ferry Pier. If arriving via the Star Ferry
   from Hong Kong, turn left as you exit and
   look for the Omni The Hong Kong Hotel
   and the entrance into Ocean Terminal just
   beside it. Ocean Terminal is one of the few
   massive shopping complexes we recommend
   you even peek at. There are another three
   miles of Harbour City shops that connect
   Ocean Terminal, Omni The Hong Kong Hotel, Ocean Centre, Ocean Galleries, and the
   Omni Marco Polo and Omni Prince hotels.
   Wandering for miles and miles of shopping
   becomes a surrealistic experience after the
   first half hour.
     In Ocean Terminal, stop first at the infor-
   mation desk and pick up the *A-O-A Map
   Directory* to Hong Kong. We found these

maps to be invaluable resources because both the streets and building names are drawn and listed. Very often an address is impossible to see, but every building has its name prominently displayed. After leaving the information desk, go upstairs and start hoofing. There are hundreds of shops.

2. Next stop is the Jade Market, which opens at 10 A.M. and closes just after lunchtime. If you choose to take a taxi, ask the driver for the corner of Reclamation and Kansu streets, across from the Yau Ma Tei Market (a produce market building that is across the street). If taking the MTR, exit at the Nathan and Jordan roads terminal, walk past the Yue Hwa Department Store, past the Wing On Bank and Department Store, past the Hotel Fortuna, and take a left on Kansu Street. You will then see ahead of you blocks of stalls with umbrellas. These are produce vendors. The Jade Market is an enclosed area just after you pass Shanghai Street. Walk through the chicken-wire enclosure and pass around the market (approximately a hundred stalls crammed together under umbrellas). Especially take note of where the Chinese people seem to be buying. We have had our best luck following Chinese shoppers, watching how they negotiated for their jade, and then counting the money as the sale was being finalized. It sounds a little silly, but unless you are a jade expert, how else can you know the fair market value for a piece of stone? We found that the prices vary enormously for stones that look similar to an untrained eye. Once you, too, have spent a day staring at green rocks they will look enormously different, but to the first-time buyer it is very confusing. Look also for the vendors selling jade pieces for practically nothing (50¢ to $5). Sometimes you can pick up some attractive pieces of jade to combine with a larger good piece for a neck-

lace. No matter what it is you want to buy, remember that this is the time to act like you don't care, and to bargain.

3. By now you will be starving. At least we always are after visiting the Jade Market. Not only will it be after noon, but also you should be so highly stimulated by the deals you were able to make that your body will need to be refueled. If not, continue on. In either case we recommend grabbing a taxi and going to the Regent. Eat an inexpensive lunch in the downstairs Harbourside coffee shop. Our next shopping stop is the hotel itself. The shopping arcade is to the left of the center lobby as you are standing facing the harbor. There are three floors of shops. Famous names you will not want to miss are Cartier, Leonard, Bally, Chanel, Trussardi, Ascot Chang Co. (custom-made shirts), Diane Freis, etc.

4. Refreshed by such luxury, walk behind the Peninsula (or through the Peninsula for more stores) to the Sands Building, 17 Hankow Road. There are several outlets here. One of our faves is Oriental Pacific. O.P. carries private-label knit goods at incredible prices. In the summer, their cotton sweaters cost from $10 to $50. The same merchandise at a chic boutique in the United States would be three times as expensive. We know—we have made the mistake of buying it! They also carry gorgeous single- or double-ply cashmeres for men and women. There is a great Chinese department store (Chung Kiu) also in the Sands Building, on the street level. It's filled with junk and great souvenirs.

5. If you bought too much you may have to return to your hotel to stash your goods. Possibly you can leave your bags at O.P. and retrieve them after you explore Nathan Road, our next stop. As you exit the Sands Building, turn right and then left on Peking

Road. Walk three blocks to Nathan Road and turn left. Nathan Road is bargain central. We get dizzy trying to count the number of watch and camera shops along this strip. Next stop is at the Burlington Arcade (92–94 Nathan Road). Sam's Tailor is on the main floor as you enter, and is an experience you don't want to miss. If you demand more than the McDonald's of tailors, try for filet mignon at W. W. Chan, where Peter Chan is one of the Big Three (see page 201). W. W. Chan & Sons has a spacious and quiet shop where the more private client can pick out beautiful English wools for his suits and fine English cottons for his shirts. Prices are a touch more than Sam's, but you pay for the quiet!

6. Just off Nathan Road is Granville Road, which seems to be discount heaven. As you leave the Burlington Arcade, turn right and continue up Nathan Road onto Granville Road. This street is filled with jobbers and bargains.

7. Take a right on Carnarvon Road until you reach Kimberley Road. Here take a right and follow Kimberley in a U as it becomes Austin Road, then Austin Avenue, and returns to cross Nathan Road. This is the young designer section of Kowloon. Kimberley Road and Austin Avenue are lined with trendy boutiques selling the latest in Hong Kong and Japanese-designed fashions.

8. Either return to Nathan Road or grab a cab to go back to your hotel. Make your dinner plans so you can be available to go to the best night market (called the Ladies' Market) in Kowloon, at about 9:30 P.M. Whole families stroll the Ladies' Market area shopping for whatever the vendors have brought in for the night. You can take the MTR to Mong Kok and exit the subway on Argyle. Mong Kok is the stop after Yau Ma Tei.

The market is mostly on Argyle. At the market you can find Fila shirts, Japanese toys, underwear, watches, electronic goods, and knits. Just about everything manufactured can be found in some vendor's pushcart. The streets have an energy similar to that of a carnival. Even the regular stores stay open late to accommodate the crowds. And yep, those shirts cost $5 each.

Size Conversion Chart

WOMEN'S DRESSES, COATS, AND SKIRTS

American	3	5	7	9	11	12	13	14	15	16	18
Continental	36	38	38	40	40	42	42	44	44	46	48
British	8	10	11	12	13	14	15	16	17	18	20

WOMEN'S BLOUSES AND SWEATERS

American	10	12	14	16	18	20
Continental	38	40	42	44	46	48
British	32	34	36	38	40	42

WOMEN'S SHOES

American	5	6	7	8	9	10
Continental	36	37	38	39	40	41
British	3½	4½	5½	6½	7½	8½

CHILDREN'S CLOTHING

American	3	4	5	6	6X
Continental	98	104	110	116	122
British	18	20	22	24	26

CHILDREN'S SHOES

American	8	9	10	11	12	13	1	2	3
Continental	24	25	27	28	29	30	32	33	34
British	7	8	9	10	11	12	13	1	2

MEN'S SUITS

American	34	36	38	40	42	44	46	48
Continental	44	46	48	50	52	54	56	58
British	34	36	38	40	42	44	46	48

MEN'S SHIRTS

American	14½	15	15½	16	16½	17	17½	18
Continental	37	38	39	41	42	43	44	45
British	14½	15	15½	16	16½	17	17½	18

MEN'S SHOES

American	7	8	9	10	11	12	13
Continental	39½	41	42	43	44½	46	47
British	6	7	8	9	10	11	12

INDEX

About the Authors

SUZY GERSHMAN is an author and journalist who has worked in the fiber and fashion industry since 1969 in both New York and Los Angeles and has held editorial positions at *California Apparel News, Mademoiselle, Gentleman's Quarterly*, and *People* magazine, where she was West Coast Style editor. She writes regularly for *Travel and Leisure;* her essays on retailing are text at the Harvard Business School. Mrs. Gershman lives in Connecticut with her husband, author Michael Gershman, and their son. Michael Gershman also contributes to the *Born to Shop* pages.

JUDITH THOMAS is a designer who began her career working in the creative and advertising departments of Estee Lauder and Helena Rubinstein in New York. Previously she was an actress in television commercials as well as on and off Broadway. In 1973 she moved to Los Angeles where she was an art director for various studios while studying for her ASID at UCLA. She is currently involved in developing and marketing new trends in building design for MPS Systems. Mrs. Thomas lives in Pennsylvania with her husband and two children.